THE MYTH OF WHITE FRAGILITY

A Field Guide to Identifying and Overcoming the Race Grifters

Jim Hanson

World Peace Publishing

Dedicated to my love Samantha—
The one who believed in me before I believed in myself.

ISBN- 9798673907863

Cover design by: Art Painter
Library of Congress Control Number: 2018675309
Printed in the United States of America

CONTENTS

FOREWORD

I'm not a racist and you probably aren't either. But, the book White Fragility by Robin DiAngelo says I am a racist and if I say I'm not, that shows I most definitely am a racist; and, when I take offense to being called a racist that's further proof of my racism. It's crazy talk, but that's where we are today.

The premise of White Fragility is that not only am I racist, but all White people in America are, too. That's not just an evil idea, it's ironically a completely racist claim.

And it makes me mad. How dare these people, who don't even know me, call me a racist? That is a vile smear and I have every right to deny a false claim against me and so do you. DiAngelo even has the unmitigated gall to assert that our anger at this unfounded insult is evidence of her uber-smear of White Fragility. Which means we can't handle the truth of our complicity.

Wrong, it's an entirely proper reaction. It's perfectly justified Whiteous Indignation at what are quite properly thought of as fighting words. Yet the concept is spreading from the radical Left into mainstream America and we need to stop it in its tracks.

Not because it is bad to oppose racism and call it out anywhere we find it, but because it is bad to invent a new kind of racism and use it to discriminate against people because of the color of their skin. I'm shocked it's even necessary to write something so obvious.

I can't sit on the sidelines while the race grifters perpetuate a market for their over-priced snake oil by pretending to fix the problem while, in fact, ensuring the problem persists. It's quite a racket for Ms. DiAngelo and friends who are raking in fat satchels of cash feeding off Black anger and White guilt. They wave their magic wand saying Systemic Racism is the cause of all the ills, but their false narrative allows the actual causes of disparate outcomes for the Black community to continue.

I know this book will open me up to baseless accusations of racism, but I choose continued dedication to making the world a better place. I will speak hard truths in the pursuit of true equality and willingly suffer the slings and arrows of outrageous accusations in order to make a real difference. I know my heart and my lifelong commitment to the Special Forces motto "De Oppresso Liber" To Free the Oppressed.

Anti-racism training and Wokeness in general is designed to gain control over how people think and act as part of the larger plan of the activist Left to fundamentally transform the United States with stealth Socialism. Anti-Racism doesn't seem like a socialist issue but that's the beauty. They can claim to be fighting for equality for the oppressed when actually they are waging a war to impose their version of equality of outcome for all.

Brilliant when you think about it since only the most vile people would stand against equality. And while most people assume they mean equal opportunity, these social engineers are muttering equal outcomes under their breath. Which is a horrible totalitarian idea and patently impossible. Socialism is all about fixing inequalities though, so it requires them to take another run at the perpetually failing slogan from societal self-help guru Karl Marx:

> "From each according to his ability, to each according
> to his needs"[1]

Penalizing the productive destroys their incentive to work

harder, so they work less hard. But our ever-idealistic friends on the Left keep assuming they will create the un-selfish humans who ignore that to properly implement "real Socialism". Let's be honest, they're doing pretty well at pushing it on us right here, right now. So, we must fight back.

This first book in the Freedom Manual Series— Defeating the Social(ist) Justice Mob— is a rhetorical call to arms and manual for how to win this battle for the soul of America. It is not a call to actual battle although the Left has in many ways shifted to open insurrection. We should not follow their lead, but instead use the powerful tools in the arsenal of representative democracy and what's left of our free speech in the digital town square to beat them fair and square.

The first battle we must wage is against what is termed White Fragility and its included claims America is completely infected with Systemic Racism thus all White people are beneficiaries and therefore racists. That's neither proven or true, but because of the systemic propaganda advantages the Left has in the mainstream media we are forced to debunk and then destroy this wicked but already widespread idea.

There are major disparities in the outcomes of Black people in America compared to other ethnicities. They are under-represented in many areas of achievement, like the business world, compared to their percentage of the population and over-represented in others, like prison. This is an ill worthy of all our efforts to improve on. That is what the White Fragility and the anti-racism movements say they are trying to do but in actuality they have just redefined racism making it acceptable and even encouraged to (racistly) label White people as racists based on the color of their skin. They are also fundamentally wrong in both their diagnosis of the current problems and the solutions they push.

This redefinition of racism includes the shift from active discrimination based on bias against a particular race to an invisible systemic racism that supposedly benefits White people and disadvantages Black people. On the surface, it seems like a good explanation for the disparate outcomes we see. However, the book doesn't look under the surface at all and offers no evidence beyond those disparate outcomes which is not how to resolve problems: looking at all possible root causes in order to identify real solutions.

I want all Americans to feel invested and be active in ensuring Black people have every opportunity to succeed. Claiming White Fragility is the magic bullet to accomplish this is a fantasy and this book will point out why. What will work is a hard and likely painful look in the mirror for all of us. The bias and prejudice that can lead to racism are present in all humans. The real question is how do we act on those impulses? That includes thoughts; words and actions both intentional and unintentional; and, even those one may not be aware of.

White Fragility is so appealing to those using it because they avoid having to prove discriminatory actions. They claim systemic racism is so deep in our society that even if White people aren't aware of it it's still behind the outcome differences. Voila, White people are racist because they're the beneficiaries of this. That's inaccurate, unfair and patently un-American. Even worse, the proposed solutions of ensuring equal outcomes would enshrine discrimination against one race, White people, while redefining that process away from its correct title of racism.

What a truly destructive idea and one we must work to derail. That is the purpose of this book. At the same time, we must also be actively involved in better solutions for the outcome differences of the black community that have been accurately identified. The key is to look at all the problems not just say the system is rigged.

There is a powerful lot of idiocy in the Wokeness package and I plan to bring you more of these Defeating the Social(ist) Justice

Mob guides.

First, we must make sure we don't enshrine a new form of racism as a feel-good solution to the historical form we have mostly eradicated. On to debunking the Myth of White Fragility.

—Jim

INTRODUCTION WAKE
UP TO WOKENESS

George Orwell was close with his book 1984, but he didn't have the imagination of today's Social Justice Warriors. He warned us about the danger of a totalitarian society that controlled all aspects of our lives and produced an always evolving ideology which if violated constituted a thoughtcrime. A key technique was Doublethink.

> The keyword here is blackwhite. Like so many Newspeak words, this word has two mutually contradictory meanings. Applied to an opponent, it means the habit of impudently claiming that black is white, in contradiction of the plain facts. Applied to a Party member, it means a loyal willingness to say that black is white when Party discipline demands this.[2]

The Wokeness and anti-racism activists have adopted this to redefine racism. They keep the original meaning of bias and discrimination by one race against another then claim only White people can do it.

They have adopted Orwell's dystopian tale as a playbook rather than a warning. White Fragility is one of their creations to implement doublethink and fight the disparate outcomes of Blacks in society by imposing discrimination against White people based on the color of their skin. Hmmmm, sounds oddly familiar and...unjust and...racist.

What you're getting here is a handbook for surviving and defeating these race grifters and jack-booted Thought Police and the limousine Liberals and skateboard Socialists who are part of their mob. And if you think you're somehow immune, you better check because your supposed White Privilege doesn't give you immunity from attack. Unless you have Jeff Bezos money, you are in the crosshairs. If you say or do the wrong thing in public or private, you can be cancelled from your job, your social circles, and soon enough put on trial for a hate crime.

The methodology of these totalitarian wannabes of the Left is Wokeness — the condition of agreeing with whatever dogma the mob is currently obsessing about. It could be racism, or trans gender rights or climate change. But whatever it is, everyone, including you, must agree and join with them to eradicate or fundamentally transform it. Sitting politely on the sidelines is no longer an option. "Silence is Violence" is literally one of their catch phrases.

Whatever the outrage du jour is, Wokeness comes with one overarching belief: America is irredeemably bad and must be remade. To be safely Woke, you must revere this single tenet regardless of all the evidence to the contrary. Ignore the fact America is far and away the freest and most prosperous place anyone of any race, creed, color, gender, sexual orientation or religion (did I skip anything? It's tough keeping up) has ever lived.

This is hardly a new thing. It is social engineering with an added twist from the folks who brought you participation trophies because everyone's a winner. Their new mandate is ensuring equal outcomes. They are not content to simply redistribute wealth, they want to slice and dice every segment of society to ensure it has the proper numbers, according to them, of all the approved identity groups. Karl Marx points out the necessity of this.

> A house may be large or small; as long as the neighboring houses are likewise small, it satisfies all social

requirement for a residence. But let there arise next
to the little house a palace, and the little house
shrinks to a hut. The little house now makes it clear
that its inmate has no social position at all to maintain.[3]

This can be called affirmative action or diversity but in the end
it's quotas. If the percentage of Black people in America is 13.6%,
then every avenue of human endeavor better have 13.6% Black
people and if not, then the people holding those slots must be
pushed aside. It matters not how many Black people are actually
interested in becoming say corporate tax auditors — meet the
quota or pay the price.

Once we start down the road of ensuring equal outcomes, totalitarian authority is the only way to achieve it. Don't doubt for
a second that massively increasing state power and control isn't a
highly desired feature of social(ist) justice. The Left wants to run
our lives because they don't like the choices we make. The Woke
Mob is in full furor right now showing us a taste of what is to come
if we don't shut 'em down.

The current cause celebre is anti-racism but in the same way
Antifa is an organization claiming to be anti-fascist while em-
ploying all the tactics and techniques of fascism. Anti-racism
consists largely of indoctrinating White people into believing
they are racist simple because they are White. Amazing really, to
discriminate against an entire group of people based on the color
of their skin. If only there was a word to describe that evil.

Aha, there is. So, their first trick redefines racism so it no longer
means beliefs and actions based on bias and prejudice against
members of another race. The new racism is the unavoidable advantage for White people based on the accumulation of centuries
of rule-making and system-building that generates White privilege and creates a White supremacist state damaging to Black
people.

This leaves all White people unable to escape the systemic racism that produces their unearned reward. Any attempt to do good works simply proves you have not accepted the inescapable nature of this insidious evil. Get used to circular reasoning and logical fallacies because they form the main framework of the ideology and methodology of White Fragility. Posit a premise with no factual basis like systemic racism, state your theology is based on its existence which is simply to be accepted, and then say refusal to accept this is proof that you suffer from the root cause, Whiteness, and benefit from the White supremacist systems in place.

There is no escape except submission and even then, you are required to atone for your original sin of being born White. You must actively join in the anti-racist dismantling of this evil, which since it permeates everything, means America must be destroyed then rebuilt in the image of Wokeness. You must attempt to influence all in your orbit of friends, family, co-workers, etc. to join or be considered part of the problem — an unrepentant racist.

The reason this madness is now so widespread is like all totalitarian ideologies, it is taught to the young and they become its shock troops and enforcers. The education system shifted long ago to leftist indoctrination factories. There are widespread pushes for woke young people to confront their parents and inform them that if they don't comply, they will be forced to inform on them. The KGB and Stasi may sue them for copyright infringement of their playbooks and Mao Zedong wholeheartedly approves.

> Cadres are a decisive factor, once the political line
> is determined. Therefore, it is our fighting task to
> train large numbers of new cadres in a planned way.
> [4]

The key to White Fragility is contained in the title epithet, which claims White people react poorly when informed they are unavoidably racist and questioning this is further proof of just how deep their racism runs. The fragility is revealed by their resistance to being tagged with the most powerful smear in our country today. I'm dizzy from all the circular reasoning.

You will be confronted with the book White Fragility in some way — at work, through your kids schools, or from that overly-educated but underly-informed relative at a family gathering. There are now consequences in many situations for refusal to engage, even worse for those who actively oppose it. I've created this guide to surviving the emissaries of the Ministry of Wokeness wherever you run into them and joining the counter-revolution to defeat them.

If you can't fight them actively, you can use the explanations of their dogma and its underlying lack of anything underlying it to go along only as much as needed. If you can fight, then I'll provide figurative hand-loaded, match-grade sniper rounds to take down its arguments and precision strike munitions to obliterate its unhealthy and unwarranted attempts to tear this country down.

And best of all, we'll get this done in one quarter the time it would take to read the drivel in White Fragility. Less if you count the multiple times you would throw it against the wall screaming "This is garbage!" while trying to read it. I took one for the team and you are the beneficiary. You owe me.

Absolutely necessary disclaimer for the people who will completely misconstrue this into some support for racism. It is NOT. I abhor racism and any discrimination based on characteristics that people cannot control. I believe slavery is an egregious stain on America and the various forms of bias, discrimination and racism that have been used over the years were wrong. In the greatness of America and the system created by our Founders we have continued our pursuit of equality and opportunity for all. Institutional racism was properly outlawed decades ago and in almost every case eradicated.

I also believe the America described in White Fragility does not exist as portrayed. The problems with disparate outcome for Blacks in many fields of endeavor and interaction with institutions in this country are very real and represent a priority to fix. However, the descriptions and solutions of White Fragility will not only fail to solve them, they will almost certainly make them worse.

This book is a guide to surviving and defeating White Fragility and the anti-racism agenda. Before we dig all the way into that, we need to note the larger goal: This isn't about stopping police violence, it is covert socialism disguised as social justice. Not surprising when you consider that Patrisse Cullors says she and her Black Lives Matter co-founder Alicia Garza "are trained Marxists". One of their stated goals right on their website says,

> "We disrupt the Western-prescribed nuclear family structure requirement by supporting each other as extended families and "villages" that collectively care for one another, especially our children, to the degree that mothers, parents, and children are comfortable."

And they certainly follow Marx's prescription for destruction of the status quo.

> "...this revolution is necessary, therefore, not only because the ruling class cannot be overthrown in any other way, but also because the class overthrowing it can only in a revolution succeed in ridding itself of all the muck of ages and become fitted to found society anew."[5]

It's not like the Left hasn't been shaking the Socialism tambourine in public. Bernie Sanders was pulling down a third of the vote in 2020 Democrat primaries. Alexandria Ocasio-Cortez has been evangelizing on the glories of the social democrat way with tremendous zeal and very little logic but she has brought many converts to the cause. They are the rising power in the Democrat party and they aren't kidding about fundamentally transforming the United States into a socialist bleep-hole.

They are all deeply hypnotized by the "no one has tried real socialism" canard. Most of them are too young and poorly over-educated to understand how it has been tried and always crashes and burns when you rely on people being willing to work harder for less, and less. Ever hopeful, they are currently designing their propaganda posters and preparing to storm the barricades for what they see as a glorious revolution. The rest of us see it as it truly is, an attempt by the least-productive sector, multi-degreed academics and the Woke Mob to destroy the goose that lays the golden eggs they are hell bent on redistributing.

So, the answer is no, you can't play socialism with your friends here. Go find some less successful country without an iron-clad Constitution that expressly forbids it and was wise enough to make sure we are armed to stop you if you get out of control.

The thing to remember in all of this is Wokeness is the stealthy path to Socialism; and, Social Justice is just the Communist Manifesto + Climate Change.

The most confused people in the world must be the Hong Kong democracy protesters. They're waving American flags while risking their lives or the real possibility of torture and life in a prison camp while they see a bunch of radical activists and trustafarian rich kids burning American flags in the freest country ever on Earth. Both are literally fighting for what the other one has.

The Hong Kong protesters want freedom, liberty and democracy. The shock troops of Wokeness want state control, thought police, and yes, socialism. Wouldn't it be a wonderful Twilight

Zone episode if they all Woke up in the other's shoes?

The current mayhem over police violence is just a means to an end. Once they stop crime by stopping the police from arresting people in Black communities and everyone lives happily in that Shangri La, they will move on to the rest of their demands. Most of these would be very recognizable to Vladimir Lenin or Mao Zedong and their tactics would bring a tear of joy to the eye of Josef Stalin.

They start by promising to right the wrong of different outcomes between Blacks and Whites. The rub is they are not interested in what causes the difference, because according to them they already know: It's Systemic Racism and they have a solution. Just change all the systems where Black people are at a disadvantage so they aren't any more.

Ta Da! Problem solved. That is the key to most of their cunning plan for America. Simply burn it all down and build new systems that give the equal outcome they require. The irony of fixing what they claim is racism that benefits Whites with what would be racism that benefits Blacks escapes them. Largely because for the ideologues who are running this show, the racial aspect is just the shiny penny right now. They want the absolute power to choose outcomes for all of us. Reward their friends and punish the thought criminals.

Class warfare is another key component of both Socialism and Wokeness. The irony again is that many of the disparate outcomes for Blacks they hold up as proof of systemic racism are much better explained as differences of class between rich and poor.

There are more poor Black people as a percentage of the population and most of the things they point out to show racism affecting Black performance are better correlated with being poor. The question then becomes, "Why are more Black people poor?" While racism is certainly a factor, there are others like dropping out of school and not living in a two-parent household which cross racial boundaries and act as predictors for being poor for everyone. Blacks do have much larger numbers who have no father in the home and who don't complete high school and those things lead to poverty.

A key point again is the Woke Mob doesn't want to identify and fix root causes. They call that blaming the victim. They want equality of outcome and they need state power to accomplish it. But they are up against some major difficulties because of that whole equal protection under the law thing in the Constitution: the 14th Amendment[7]

In more of this unending irony, the America they want to dismantle is the same America that was designed so we eventually could stop institutional racism against Black people and all other minorities. Now it gets in the way of creating equal outcomes because it's pretty tough to pick winners and losers based on race without going afoul of equal protection, which was the whole point of having it.

The power to deliver equal outcomes is the first step down the Wokeness path to stealth Socialism. They will not stop there because people do all kinds of things with that pesky liberty that the Left does not approve of and they will strip us of it for our own good. This brings us to another key aspect of Woke socialism: They believe the Great UnWoke cannot be allowed to run their own lives.

Climate hysteria was pushed out of the way as systemic racism polled better with the rioting mobs. The choice of a particular grievance doesn't matter as long as they can get the mob rolling. But underneath, as Orwell reminded us, the image of a boot stamping on a human face — forever is waiting when they fully achieve their totalitarian dreams.

They would not agree about wanting actual totalitarianism, but, there is no way to achieve their goals without it. People are not going to un-selfishly sell their SUV, remove their air-conditioning, and walk to work just because Greta Thunberg is stressed out. They would call their paradise benevolent socialism. "From each according to their ability to each according to their needs" because you are Woke and see the rightness of this, not because we are pointing the giant gun of state power at you.

And once they get that power they will use it and be loathe to give it up as Chairman Mao noted:

> "Don't you want to abolish state power?" Yes, we do, but not right now. We cannot do it yet. Why? Because imperialism still exists, because domestic reaction still exists, because classes still exist in our country.[8]

Things will never be equal enough for the Woke mob, and if we let them have that power they'll never give it up.

The Myth of White Fragility is written with the chapters split in a purposeful way. The first section, Bottom Line Up Front, gives the common-sense layman terms look at how to understand what the White Fragility cabal is up to and what it means to you. The second section, the Deep Dive, takes specific analytical aim at the claims of the book and debunks them with the context White Fragility is sorely lacking. The third section, Calls to Action, identifies substantive ways to get into and support this fight.

This is still mostly an information war so much of the action will be tactics and techniques for talking about all this without stepping on any land mines. It's vital we use the revulsion most Americans feel for the rioting, looting and destruction of our heritage to bring them to our side and consolidate enough political power to stop this. Next in the seriess we will get to the vital steps of saving free speech, our right to be an armed citizenry, fundamentally transforming our education system, ensuring Greta

Thunberg and her climate goons don't destroy our economy and countering the cultural rot that comes out of Hollywood with quality alternatives.

We have a lot to do. First let's win this battle of ideas on racism.

Feel free to skip around in the denser parts of the Deep Dives to pick and choose what interests you. It is there to provide an understanding of the flaws of the book and specific points to refute them. Helpful if you want to use their own supposed facts against them. Now it's time to ruck-up and march to the sounds of gunfire.

CHAPTER ONE
FOUNDATIONS OF FRAGILITY

Bottom Line Up Front

White Fragility says America is plagued by systemic racism which causes lower outcomes for Black people compared to other races. This systemic racism infects all White people even if they can't identify it or deny it about themselves; and, infects all our institutions. Everyone must accept this and work to dismantle and remake America or be punished and cast out.

This is part of the agenda of Wokeness we are all faced with as the Leftist mob works to fundamentally transform this country. They are done playing around and the presidency of Donald Trump did us all a big favor as they ripped the masks off and started admitting, "Yes, we really do hate America and we want to burn it down then build a socialist and social justice paradise."

They are showing their true colors. Good. Previously, they worked on many of the same goals, but hid it much better. They're done with a long term marketing campaign and are going to just shove it down our throats.

The White Fragility game is part of their larger pursuit of

Socialism here in America. Although the radicals are totally on board, the Left is not fully united on the topic of Socialism. If they were, Bernie Sanders would have been their presidential nominee in 2016 and again in 2020, but in both races the Democrats voted for non-socialists. Although he did make a pretty strong run this time around until the Democrat party pulled the rug out from under him with their Super Tuesday shenanigans.

Since direct election didn't work to get their totalitarian regime in place, the activists have shifted to pushing equal outcomes as a stepping-stone on the path to total control. While they didn't get the nomination, the Bernie and AOC wing has already coopted the Biden campaign. They are driving the train; he's just sitting in the observation car watching the lovely trees go by.

They long ago took over education and began indoctrinating kids with Leftist propaganda instead of teaching them. They own our entertainment and culture industries and have been using it to push their worldview for decades. White Fragility & Wokeness is spreading like COVID-19 and infecting millions.

There are many things they want to change but right now racism is the top seller since little Greta Thunberg and AOC were unable to convince us to kill all the cows and cars and walk out to the meadow to eat grass ourselves.

White Fragility is stunningly bold. It claims, without any actual proof, that all White people and all the systems that run this country are racist…to the bone. And the really twisted thing author Robin DiAngelo does is say if you don't agree with this, it's just more proof of how racist you are. Brilliant. There is no way out.

The solution she demands, and the thought police of anti-racism training will enforce, is to admit your racist roots, accept your guilt and help them tear everything down. Failure to comply is not an option and the mob will come for anyone clinging to their thoughtcrimes. Orwell would be impressed with their audacity.

CHAPTER 1- DEEP DIVE

"White people in North America live in a society that
is deeply separate and unequal by race, and White
people are the beneficiaries of that separation and
inequality" Pg. 1 White Fragility[9]

That is the thesis of White Fragility. The solution is to have all
White people admit their culpability and guilt and to remake all
institutions to ensure equal outcomes. The author says that progress can begin:

"only after we accept that racism is unavoidable and
that it is impossible to completely escape having
developed problematic racial assumptions and be-
haviors." Pg. 4 White Fragility[10]

Neither the thesis or her proposed solution is supported by
evidence, statistics, or analysis that would be acceptable to any
academic or professional paper or serious book. But that is not
what it is. It is a political playbook for transferring power and
control over society to the activist Left. It uses race as the most
effective way to begin this fundamental transformation, but she
explicitly states that this is part of a larger movement.

"This book is unapologetically rooted in identity politics" Pg. xiv introduction White Fragility[11]

That is not a shocking revelation, but it should cause us to
evaluate her prescriptions with the understanding that racial disparities are not the sole flaw that must be overcome.

"The term identity politics refers to the focus on the
barriers specific groups face in their struggle for

equality." Pg. xiii introduction White Fragility[12]

Sure, but it has also become the mechanism where the chosen identity groups of the Left exercise power in the pursuit of equity, not just equality. It is the basis for a type of spoils system to begin the redistribution of wealth and there is no question where the wealth will be redistributed from.

> "The identities of those sitting at the tables of power
> in this country have remained remarkably similar:
> White, male, middle- and upper-class, able-bodied."
> Pg. xiii White Fragility[13]

Let me state categorically that the bias, prejudice and discrimination exercised by White men throughout the history of this country is indisputable and indefensible. I am neither denying it or minimizing it in making the critiques that follow. I do, however, challenge the premise that America is currently a White supremacist country and that systemic racism benefitting White people and disadvantaging Black people exists in the way Ms. DiAngelo claims. Furthermore, the solutions she proposes are actually counter-productive to the goal of increasing sustainable achievement and outcomes in the Black community.

The primary type of faulty logic and my main criticism of White Fragility is it uses disparate outcomes for Blacks as essentially the entire basis to support the claim of systemic racism. She cites plenty of statistics that show the gaps between Whites and Blacks in financial and professional success; and, highlights the clearly unequal numbers of arrests and convictions of Blacks in the justice system. However, disparate outcomes alone cannot support the conclusion that this novel concept known as systemic racism is the causative factor.

Once it is established these disparate outcomes exist, conducting an impartial examination of all possible correlative factors is essential if finding sustainable solutions is, in fact, the goal. It is crucial to be very careful to avoid claims that even factors with high correlation are necessarily causative.

Security Studies Group conducted an analysis of one of the main claims of the Black Lives Matter movement, that there is an epidemic of police shootings of unarmed Blacks and systemic racism in policing is the cause.

There was no question that Blacks were killed and arrested in larger numbers than their percentage of the population, but, we found there was little to no proof that systemic racism was the cause and that a number of other factors are much more highly related.

> "Our findings show there has been no increase in total
> number of police homicides or percentage of Blacks
> killed in them. We also found that race does not
> correlate as well as other factors, specifically: (1)At-
> tacking a police officer or civilian, (2) the sex of the
> victim being male, and (3) the amount of violent
> crime in the victim's neighborhood."[14]

Much of the furor fueling the current unrest and the faulty conclusion police racism is the cause is based on this collection of anomalies without doing any of the analysis, as we did. Yet a basic look at the most definitive statistics shows this is not a reasonable or even likely conclusion. This should prompt a much deeper evaluation of exceedingly broad claims like those made by Ms. DiAngelo of a systemic racism so pervasive that America as a whole is a White supremacist country.

> "Race scholars use the term White supremacy to
> describe a sociopolitical economic system of dom-
> ination based on racial categories that benefits
> those defined and perceived as White. This system
> of structural power privileges, centralizes, and
> elevates White people as a group." Pg. 30 White

Fragility[15]

She then goes on to note a number of disparate outcomes showing Blacks inequitably represented in positions of influence. That is certainly something worth investigating to determine potential causes and solutions. But again, disparate outcomes are not prima facie evidence of systemic racism or a White supremacist society as the cause. There is no consideration of any other factors that could contribute to this and the supporting citations are mainly opinions

> "In Ta-Nehisi Coates's essay "The Case for Reparations," he makes a similar point:
>
> To ignore the fact that one of the oldest republics in the world was erected on a foundation of White supremacy, to pretend that the problems of a dual society are the same as the problems of unregulated capitalism, is to cover the sin of national plunder with the sin of national lying. The lie ignores the fact that reducing American poverty and ending White supremacy are not the same. . . . [W]hite supremacy is not merely the work of hotheaded demagogues, or a matter of false consciousness, but a force so fundamental to America that it is difficult to imagine the country without it." Pg. 30 White Fragility[16]

This is a purely rhetorical argument and while perfectly suitable for making, as he does, a case for a desired policy such as reparations, it provides no analytical underpinning for the huge supposition that America currently represents a racist and White supremacist entity. And you won't find any better arguments anywhere else in the book. It's just rhetoric on top of differentials in achievement.

The proclamation of giant concepts based on the time-honored, but fundamentally flawed, proof that a lot of smart people agree with me is the main technique of White Fragility. She posits the following non-scientifically or analytically supported propositions in the book.

> A. Systemic Racism exists in American institutions and benefits Whites to the detriment of Blacks.
> B. Racism is only possible when those in power i.e. Whites are prejudiced against those not in power i.e. Blacks.
> C. Whites are inherently racist and often in denial or unable to perceive their White privilege.
> D. The combination of these things has created a White supremacist state in the U.S.
> E. White Fragility is the reaction when White people are presented with this and try to avoid responsibility.

All of these were established by noting disparate outcome and then simply pronouncing some flavor of racism alone as the cause. She then moves on to the prescription for what ails us, which is White people admitting their racism even if and especially if they cannot comprehend having any. The systemic racism she invented asserts White people benefit even without their active participation, so there is no escaping the mantle of racist. This is another example of circular reasoning paired with a requirement to atone for things you haven't done and don't even think.

White Fragility is an excellent model for Social Justice warfare. It requires no proof. You simply take a pre-conceived notion, claim it exists, then move right on to steamrolling the world to fit your predetermined outcome. Well that's not how we do things here, and it's time Ms. DiAngelo and her crew find that out.

CHAPTER 1- CALLS TO ACTION

(The image is a V for Victory which will annoy the Left because they think it's a peace sign.) You took the first step by buying and reading this book. Here are some others:

Scrub your back trail.

Everyone says and does questionable things so look to see what may be in your searchable past. The second you get into this game and start fighting back against the Left's tyrannical pursuit of totalitarian control, the other side will come after you. Google yourself. Search your social media history. If there is anything you don't want to have to explain at a PTA meeting, get rid of it. Some obsessed loser will find that time you called someone fat, made fun of someone's hair, or some other insensitive thing you said 37 years ago. Don't give them ammo to hurt you with.

Start recruiting for our team.

Odds are you're doing some of this already, but take it to the next level. Examine your sphere of influence and think about who is open to the idea that maybe America should not be destroyed in order to fix her. Talk to them calmly, rationally, and with facts at your disposal.

Find where White Fragility is used.

It may be your kid's school, your office, or local or state government. When you locate it, push back.

Don't let them get away with using their propaganda as a training guide.

Identify what resonates with you.

Highlight the points in White Fragility and the reality checks here that impact you the most. Read up some more on those, check source materials, be relentlessly informed because the attacks on you will be savage. Knowledge is power.

CHAPTER TWO
SYSTEMIC RACISM

Bottom Line Up Front

Systemic Racism claims centuries of White creation and domination of the processes and institutions that run America created an interlocking system that favors Whites and damages Blacks. The "systemic" part means it doesn't require any actual act of discrimination or even any visible means of achieving its nefarious goals just that Blacks and Whites overall have different outcomes in multiple areas.

This is another bold move that eliminates the need to prove racist actions or intent by anybody. It's so deep in the system that it can't even be seen. You have to respect the guts it takes to throw something that outrageous out there. It truly saves a lot of time studying actual root causes when you can just say "Black youths get arrested three times as much as White youths, therefore racism" without looking at many studies[17] that show plenty of factors that are more likely causes than racism.

It helps to get the result you want when you skip more than half the scientific process. Especially when that pesky analysis completely destroys the whole premise. Racism must be "systemic" because when looked for it can't be found. There have to be plenty of really smart people on the Left watching this saying, "Dang, I can't believe they are getting away with that" but they like the result and are not about to rock the boat.

Let me state categorically and without reservation (again) that disparate outcomes for Black people are a real problem and deserve our attention. VOX is an excellent go-to source for bad and dishonest use of information as propaganda supporting Leftist causes. It would be a shame not to use their stuff to show how this game is played. There are a whole slew of graphs at the link showing:

> "All this is a reminder that there are chronic and interconnected factors that exclude black Americans from the benefits of a strong economy, and cause them more anguish than Americans of other ethnicities — particularly white Americans — when times are bad. And although they are so tangled that it is difficult to tell precisely where one economic issue begins and another ends, it is clear they all have one source: the systemic racism that has devalued black labor for more than four centuries and the social injustices that have stemmed from it."

Ta Da, that is sheer perfection in policy propaganda.

> "although they are so tangled that it is difficult to tell precisely where one economic issue begins and another ends"

Translation: We have zero proof or even correlation. But let's not let lack of evidence detour our desired end state: "it is clear they all have one source: the systemic racism".

Shameless hackery of the first order. The cause demands they ignore a major tenet of statistical analysis and flip the actual rule on its head, taking it from correlation is not causation to correlation is causation because...racism. It's the magic ingredient in all this alchemy.

Replacing institutional racism like segregated lunch counters, which have been banned in the U.S. for decades, with systemic racism which doesn't need to be validated and can't even be measured makes their next steps so much easier. Every time they need a cause for a problem, just cite systemic racism. It works for everything. It needs its own infomercial:

"Have you been wasting your time looking for root causes to the toughest social problems in this country?

Your days of open inquiry and rigorous analysis are over. Presenting the all-purpose, one size fits all, cause of all that ails you: Systemic Racism.
Got a problem with arrest rates? Systemic Racism.
Too few Black people on TV? Systemic Racism.
Somebody make fun of your hair? Systemic Racism".

It would be sad if they weren't actually getting away with it. But now the phrase is bandied about by all kinds of expert hucksters on TV and in the newspapers. It serves as the evil that inspired protesters, rioters and looters to fill the streets, destroy property, attack innocent victims in some cases resulting in murder. They consider themselves righteously justified. It is perverse. They claim the system is fixed, there's no way they can get a fair shake, so they riot, pillage and burn because, hey, taking a few flat screens is their right. Right? No, it simply is not.

The long-term danger now, aside from imminent physical and social danger, is violence worked. Major changes in policing and other areas are being made to satiate the mob although none of the problems being fixed are identified beyond the generic place-holder of systemic racism.

Of course, there is an element of racism that affects Black people in America, but that reality is not cause to simply say "Eureka!" while moving straight to dismantling and rebuilding the country. Racism, bias, and prejudice are blights on the human condition and occur in all people, meaning in all directions, and no one has blanket immunity from these perils.

As members of the human race, we are all susceptible to these harmful attributes and need to examine our thoughts, actions, and motives to ensure a fair and just society. There are no scientific reasons for Black achievement to be less than White achievement. Even though systemic racism is a nice fit to explain the difference between White and Black achievement, that doesn't mean it does and doesn't make it the all-purpose fix.

This will not be easy, so strap in for a long haul.

CHAPTER 2- DEEP DIVE

Systemic Racism is a truly ground-shifting creation since Institutional Racism, like banning Blacks from entry to a particular college, is not just illegal it is essentially non-existent. Systemic Racism was invented and is being used to explain disparate outcomes or the difference in satisfaction between White and Black people about the institutions of this country like business, finance, and criminal justice. Getting a viable, useful, or clear definition of it is problematic.

National NAACP President Derrick Johnson is widely quoted defining it as:

> "systems and structures that have procedures or processes that disadvantages African Americans."[18]

Glenn Harris, president of Race Forward and publisher of Colorlines, called it

> "the complex interaction of culture, policy and institutions that holds in place the outcomes we see in our lives."[19]"

Both of these simply establish the definition as: Whatever systems, institutions, or people exist where disparate outcomes are found. That is not a definition, it is circular reasoning. American institutions are the cause of systemic racism because they cause disparate outcomes which is claimed, without proof, as evidence of systemic racism. That is not how this works, not how any of this works.

There are widely available and legitimate datasets showing that Blacks achieve at diminished levels in all of these areas in comparison to other races. There is also considerable polling data showing Blacks trust these institutions far less and believe they are disadvantaged by them thus creating a negative self-ful-filling prophecy.

A common theme in media discussion of this topic is to say, as this piece does with a headline that challenges:

> "If you don't believe systemic racism is real, explain
>   these statistics"[20]

And then they present these mostly undisputed examples of disparate outcomes followed by an "a ha" claim that a supposed inability to dispute them is proof of their validity as causation of systemic racism.

Again, not how any of this works. Regardless of the seemingly nice fit between Black achievement issues and racism as the cause, the burden of proof rests with the one making the assertion. Requiring others to disprove the claim without first having proved the point is ludicrous.

In addition, there is a lot of widely available data that brings into play many other potential root causes for the gap in Black achievement like this study from the Heritage Foundation.

The Real Root Causes of Violent Crime: The Breakdown of Marriage, Family, and Community

> "children born into single-parent families are much
>   more likely than children of intact families to fall
>   into poverty and welfare dependence themselves
>   in later years...While this link between illegitim-
>   acy and chronic welfare dependency now is better
>   understood, policymakers also need to appreciate
>   another strong and disturbing pattern evident in
>   scholarly studies: the link between illegitimacy and
>   violent crime and between the lack of parental at-

tachment and violent crime"[21]

Or this study from the Manhattan Institute's Glenn Loury, who happens to be Black.

Why Does Racial Inequality Persist? Culture, Causation, and Responsibility

> "Over the last 40 years, I've explored why, notwith-
> standing the success of the civil rights movement,
> the subordinate status of African-Americans per-
> sists. Key to my thinking about this intractable
> problem has been the need to distinguish the role
> played by discrimination against Black people from
> that played by counterproductive behavioral pat-
> terns among Blacks....
>
> This puts what is a very sensitive issue rather starkly. Many vocal advocates for racial equality have been loath to consider the possibility that problematic patterns of behavior could be an important factor contributing to our persisting disadvantaged status. Some observers on the right of American politics, meanwhile, take the position that discrimination against Blacks is no longer an important determinant of unequal social outcomes. I have long tried to chart a middle course—acknowledging anti-Black biases that should be remedied while insisting on addressing and reversing the patterns of behavior that impede Black people from seizing newly opened opportunities to prosper."
> "[22]

But these studies and the attendant data on school achievement and spending along with data and analytics about Black crime are not helpful to the narrative that systemic racism is the cause. This contrary information is mostly ignored or, and here is another key tactic, described as racist.

That an achievement gap exists is proven, that it can be attributed to the nebulous and seemingly indefinable concept of systemic racism is not. The proper response to the achievement gap is to take a systematic look at all factors that can lead to a difference in outcomes. Simply assigning racism as the causative evil that must be eradicated is not just improper, but quite likely to allow the other factors to persist, therefore allowing disparate outcomes to continue. It creates the assumption the problem has been solved when it has not.

The other pathologies identified in the Black community have been shown to correlate with lack of success. Placing the blame on systemic racism while failing to fully study the actual extent of effect the other factors have is to treat a symptom without bothering to diagnose the disease.

Polling data showing that Blacks distrust institutions is fairly clear to the extent it means Black people believe they are disadvantaged in their interactions with institutions. They have been in the past and continue to be told this by the Left and in their own communities. It's reasonable they believe it at face value especially when disparate outcomes are cited as proof of the oppression that validates their distrust of institutions. The recent protests are a good example.

> "Similar shares of Black adults point to longstanding concerns about the treatment of Black people and anger over George Floyd's death as major factors underlying the protests (83% and 81%, respectively, say each of these factors contributed a great deal). In addition, 76% of Black adults say tensions between Black people and the police have contributed a great deal to the protests."[23]

The belief in what is now called systemic racism has been building for a long time and while the fear, pain, anger, and resentment felt by the Black community are absolutely real, they are often based on the same disparate outcomes methodology and therefore not necessarily indicative of the real problems. This is exceptionally damaging to race relations and the overall functioning of our civil society and culture.

Slavery and racism have caused long-term damage resulting in a legacy passed down through generations of Black people as an inheritance of injustice. I don't question the validity of those things and I mourn their occurrence. We can all acknowledge that and while those alive today don't bear responsibility, we can offer sympathy and a helping hand.

But, when large segments of the populace believe that there is currently a problem like systemic racism and it is the cause of poor outcomes for Blacks, we all suffer for that belief. If it was proven, then the sentiment and energy for radical changes that are currently being pushed would be entirely warranted, but it is not proven. Therefore, a false sense of pain and fear over this has been perpetuated. Undoubtedly, racism exists and it negatively impacts Black people. But it doesn't stop there. It's an evil that disperses in all directions and there is no person or group of people immune from it. The creation of systemic racism as a lurking wickedness peculiar to White people that explains achievement gaps unfairly focuses the spotlight on something not even legitimately identified.

Misdiagnosing an ailment is catastrophic and the same is true when you apply a supposed miracle cure like White Fragility which does nothing to fix actual factors responsible for the difference in outcomes. Pointing this out is characterized by White Fragility as a rejection of both the problems that exist and any personal or collective responsibility as a White person. It's really more caring and shows a deeper level of true concern and desire for equality to point out the fallacies of this and other issues of faulty information knowing fully that the Left will attack with a vengeance. Only when we seek to identify reasons for the problems the Black community is experiencing today will we be able to make sustainable changes. Only then can we be certain everything we can do is being done. Simply going along with the mis-diagnosis does nothing to deal with the larger set of problems.

A side element in White Fragility is the notion that race and racial identity is a recent invention that was created to solidify White supremacy.

> "Race is an evolving social idea that was created to
> legitimize racial inequality and protect White ad-
> vantage." Pg. 17 White Fragility[24]

Race and ethnicity are an exceedingly complex field of study and without attempting to square the circles between them, identity groups have always been an essential part of human interaction. Some type of fear of "the other" is one of the most basic survival instincts. Starting with the family group and ex-tending to the tribe and then various levels of governance and na-tional identity, for good or bad, is how humans organize.

The idea that this was done uniquely in the nascent United States to achieve a dominant position for Whites is absurd.

The Chinese created the Han identity out of an interest in building both a cohesive nation that included the groups they deemed as part of the Han and excluding those who they did not like including the Mongols and other groups.

Critical Han Studies, The History, Representation, and Identity of China's Majority

> "Yet if one were to search for an explanation as to why
> Han "ethnicity" has so far eluded careful scholarly
> examination, this might well be because, as the
> dominant group, the Han were by definition denied
> the possibility of being ethnic at all."[25]

In an oddly ironic way, this parallels the current state of racial and ethnic affairs in the United States. The New York Times is considered a major source of news and opinion and they recently changed their stylebook policies on punctuation. They will now capitalize Black when referring to the group of people culturally known as Blacks because in the words of their senior editors:

Uppercasing Black

> "we've decided to adopt the change and start using uppercase "Black" to describe people and cultures of African origin, both in the United States and elsewhere. We believe this style best conveys elements of shared history and identity, and reflects our goal to be respectful of all the people and communities we cover."[26]

That is a partly ethnic, political and cultural choice by the New York Times and it matches their capitalization of Native and Indigenous as well as Asian-American to identify those groups. Black seems to have supplanted African-American as the most widely used term, so there is logic in making this change.

But then they explain this.

> "We will retain lowercase treatment for "White." While there is an obvious question of parallelism, there has been no comparable movement toward widespread adoption of a new style for "White," and there is less of a sense that "White" describes a shared culture and history. Moreover, hate groups and White supremacists have long favored the uppercase style, which in itself is reason to avoid it."

Another mish mash of ethnic, political and cultural concerns, but one which makes very little sense when you factor in the amount of coverage the Times gives to the concepts of:
Whiteness
White Privilege

And even
White Fragility

Apparently, they can find a common thread tying all of the Whiteness encompassed by those concepts together for censure, but not in a way that would lead to White being treated equally to Black. This is not a call for some special relevance and status for Whiteness or White people. It is simply a recognition of the incoherence on this topic among even the most elite publications.

I chose to capitalize both Black and White in this book largely because the New York Times rationale was so offensive.

Robin DiAngelo makes a brief foray into a vastly under-explored element for explaining disparate outcomes by mentioning class

> "Because race is a product of social forces, it has also
> manifested itself along class lines; poor and work-
> ing-class people were not always perceived as fully
> White." Pg. 19 White Fragility[27]

This seems like a good way to acknowledge that many of the same pathologies in the Black community that can affect success also exist in poor members of other races, but that was not her intent. She is claiming these groups were only affected by bias against their class until it suited the dominant Whites.

> "However, poor and working-class Whites were even-
> tually granted full entry into Whiteness as a way to
> exploit labor." Pg. 43 White Fragility[28]

That is truly a missed opportunity to dig into basis of achievement for all people in America as there are patterns of behavior that lead to failure or success regardless of race or ethnicity. From a Brookings Institute study came "Three simple rules poor teens should follow to join the middle class" **Ron Haskins** March 13,

2013.

    1. Graduate from high school.

    2. Maintain a full-time job or have a partner who does.

    3. Have children while married and after age 21, should they choose to become parents.

Personal responsibility is a much tougher sell than the magic bullet of systemic racism which requires no proof and no sacrifice on the part of those affected. They simply are to be rewarded for what was taken from them by this unseen, unmeasured menace.

CHAPTER 2- CALLS TO ACTION

Learn why "correlation is not causation".

It's an easy phrase to bandy about when debunking statistics, but learn why. The simple answer is that two things can track with each other but that does not show one causes the other. Example: Ice cream sales peak at the same time murders do. But it's highly unlikely the ice cream created a bunch of cold-hearted killers.

Much of White Fragility is based on taking differences in outcome between Whites and Blacks and immediately proceeding to Systemic Racism as the reason. That's cheating. In many of these cases, substituting rich and poor for Black and White results in very similar disparities and the people suffering ill effects would be both Black and White.

Dig into root causes.

Pick a disparate outcome, like percentages of people in prison by race, and deep dive into possible reasons. Have this information at hand so the next time someone wants to play the systemic racism game you can drop some knowledge on them. Using their own sources against them is sweet.

Start discussions by acknowledging realities.

Begin conversations by agreeing that disparate outcomes for Black people in this country are real and we all have an interest in trying to make them better. It can be hard to do at first, because you're often talking to a smarty pants Lefty who thinks they're morally superior to you.

You're not going to change the mind of a wild-eyed true believer, but trying to influence the other people in range is a worthy pursuit. Starting by agreeing to the validity of part of the problem signals to them you're not a zealot.

CHAPTER THREE
NEW AND MORE USEFUL DEFINITION OF RACISM

Bottom Line Up Front

Racism is no longer active discrimination by one race against another. It has been helpfully redefined to be the advantage gained by one race with more power over another one. And it applies to every member of the dominant race, in this case Whites, regardless of whether they believe in racist ideas or not. Whiteness in America is racism.

Now the first thing you probably just said is, "Well that is completely unfair". You're right. It's discrimination and bias based on skin color to make such a statement. And that is the trick they are trying to pull; racism is now a one-way street. Whites can be racist, and all of them are, but no other race can.

It is essential to the whole concept of White Fragility that they make this split. Part of the plan is to make White people feel guilty for what they have achieved since it is the result of systemic racism. Don't for a second buy into Ms. DiAngelo's claim she doesn't want people to feel guilty. It's a tactic she disingenuously uses because guilt is a vital part of getting people to admit their complicity. If they can steal your achievements, they also remove your right to judge anyone else for a lack of achievement because the whole system is rigged in your favor.

Aside from the guilt factor, they needed to be able to hold White people responsible for Black achievement in comparison even if you, or anyone else, weren't discriminating against Black people. The reason for that is there is very little of that active and open style of discrimination left anywhere. This shows up in the prevalence of fake hate crimes. Reveling in victimhood has infected our society resulting in false claims of racially motivated beatings, slur slinging, and putting a clothesline around one's neck. The country has seen an epidemic of fake hate in the absence of real hate and it's needed to fuel the outrage machine.

The new and improved racism doesn't need that. No actual hate crimes or open discrimination required. Since the entire system is racist, then all White people benefit and all Black people don't. Voila, if you are White, you're a racist.

It is also helpful to their agenda because it stops White people from being able to point out that acts of discrimination and hate by other races based on their White skin color are also racist. Especially since all groups have problems with bias and discrimination against "others". Until this redefined meaning of racism, that was...well...racism. Not now, no can do my friend, the less powerful cannot racist uphill, so these acts are downgraded and only White people can bear what is truly the most damaging smear in this country, racist.

CHAPTER 3- DEEP DIVE

"Yet our simplistic definition of racism — as intentional acts of racial discrimination committed by
immoral individuals — engenders a confidence that
we are not part of the problem and that our learning
is thus complete." Pg. 9 White Fragility[29]

She has made the leap from requiring active animus and actions based on it to the simple possession of White skin.

"We might think of Whiteness as all the aspects of
being White—aspects that go beyond mere physical
difference and are related to the meaning and result-
ant material advantage of being defined as White in
society: what is granted and how it is granted based
on that meaning. Instead of the typical focus on how
racism hurts people of color, to examine Whiteness
is to focus on how racism elevates White people."
Pg. 25 White Fragility[30]

This flips it on its head and instead of racism being an act
against Black people, it is an unwarranted bounty that is received
by White people. That is exceptionally helpful in a world where
overt acts of racism are rare. No need to show any racism because
it is there under the surface ensuring the disparate outcomes we
all agree exist.

The effort to redefine racism as only that form of racial bias
exercised by a race in a position of power toward one that is not
has been going on for a while. It is a great way for activists to be
able to attack Whites and exempt Blacks from a type of behavior
practiced by human beings regardless of specific ethnicity. The

term racist is such a powerful epithet it is helpful to be able to use it against your chosen oppressors and shield the chosen victims.

In one way, this unconscious and inevitable racism is that perfect tag. You don't have to prove it and the targets can't avoid it by not thinking or acting racist. She has even decided the act of not acting racist is...racist. The only way to react properly is to acknowledge your racism and the benefits you accrue as a member of a White supremacist society and then help her tear it all down.

Since she explicitly removes actual active racism from the White Fragility version it then allows an exemption to the bias and prejudice exhibited by the Black community and any others. Their acts of discrimination are simply bias and prejudice if it were even to come up, which it doesn't because this book is about White abuses not the pathologies shared by the entire human race. It saves the Big R only for the White folks who all deserve it.

She makes sure everyone gets the identifier by stating, as usual without any factual back up, that it is a universal wrong attributed to and enjoyed by all White people.

> "...only after we accept that racism is unavoidable and
> that it is impossible to completely escape having
> developed problematic racial assumptions and
> behaviors. None of the White people whose actions
> I describe in this book would identify as racist. In
> fact, they would most likely identify as racially
> progressive and vehemently deny any complicity
> with racism. Yet all their responses illustrate White
> fragility and how it holds racism in place. These responses spur the daily frustrations and indignities."
> Pg. 4 White Fragility[31]

You have to give her credit for the sheer boldness of making this applicable to everyone, but especially to her own subset of Whiteness, progressives. They are supposed to be the good guys, the tolerant ones, the dare I say, White saviors? And that is where she gets them. They are not allowed to do any White-knighting because they're White. It is actually counter-productive to pretend you are part of the solution when your Whiteness shows unequivocally you are the problem. Therefore, working to solve the problem exemplifies being the problem; sitting on the sidelines is racist because "Silence is Violence"; and, any and all good deeds are merely "performative".

Her attack on her own tribe is aided by the well-established liberal guilt which is mostly a White thing. Academia has been teaching this for several generations and those on the Left are quite well-prepped to put on whatever hair shirt is appropriate for the crime du jour. Her insider status makes it even harder to deny her, she's one of them and she spills the beans on everyone.

The lack of any proven connectivity between her identification of the symptom of disparate outcome and her invention of a disease that just happens to fit it is brilliant. She tailors the diagnosis and remedy to what she and all of them knew going in, it's all racism.

> "This book does not attempt to provide the solution to racism. Nor does it attempt to prove that racism exists; I start from that premise. My goal is to make visible how one aspect of White sensibility continues to hold racism in place: White fragility. Pg. 5 White Fragility[32]

The sheer chutzpah to invent a new style of uber-pervasive and invisible racism and simply start from the premise it exists and is extant in the way she describes it is stunning. And of course, she is not interested in a solution to racism.

1. It's part of human nature
2. It's her meal ticket

Especially her hybrid unavoidable version which requires lots and lots of expert training to even mitigate at all. Knowing we must try, there she is wrapping the entire package up in the nicely derogatory term White Fragility and selling the solution for exorbitant fees.

CHAPTER 3- CALLS TO ACTION

Never cave to the mob.

Start by refusing to accept being called a racist. Continue by refusing to accept their garbage new definition of racism that tries to make sure only White people can be racist. Remind them that George Orwell's book 1984 was fiction; a warning against exactly this redefining of words and ideas; and, not a road map to follow to their socialist paradise. Remind them there are no socialist paradises and never will be.

Study the real meaning of racism.

This new racism definition is an ideological one and its design is to generate a justification to place blame only on White people and exempt other races from criticism. Sociology, when uninfected by social(ist) justice, points out that all races start with an instinctive fear of the "other". It is a survival mechanism. Racism requires a value judgment that the other is bad or less than your in-group or tribe.

Refuse to budge on this regardless of their squeals that racism requires being in a position of dominance and power. Everyone wields whatever power they can and it is no less bad when done by races other than White.

Call them out for the inherently political power grab this new racism represents.

It is indoctrinated liberal Whites allied with the whole array of Identity Politics activist groups they have created trying to build a mechanism to seize control. Racism is just the shiny penny right now. Their goal is to control how we are allowed think and act. Their other social justice causes are teed up and ready to go if they pull off this coup.

CHAPTER FOUR WHITES
ARE INHERENTLY RACIST

Bottom Line Up Front

Another smart tactic in the White Fragility game is saying Whiteness is a state of being, not a belief system and therefore cannot be escaped. Living while White generates an unearned reward based solely on that fact which gives Whites an unearned advantage and at the same time Blacks an unfair disadvantage. Many White people are unable or refuse to admit this. They must be educated to see their guilt, made to feel guilty, and then to join in dismantling the system.

The term Whiteness is every bit as invented an idea as the Left claims race is overall. But it is useful to them, so they ignore that. It's a way to take all the things White people say and do and call them proof of the racist nature of both them and the system that benefits them. Makes sense if the goal is to create a sense of guilt that can't be escaped. One might think punctuality is a positive attribute but it's a White characteristic therefore racist and bad. Then it's used as proof of bias and White privilege.

Even better, here is where DiAngelo adds her Jedi Mind Trick that thinking you are not racist and acting as if you can treat people as individuals is further proof you are deeply and irredeemably racist. They reinterpret Martin Luther King Jr. for his common sense notion that his children should be judged on the content of their character not the color of their skin.

Now if you're like me you just did a stunned, "Did that White woman just erase MLK from the game?" Not completely, they just erased the common sense and brutally obvious point he made that judging people by color is bad. A color-blind world doesn't work for their messaging and plans. They need us separated by race and for all decisions to take that into account. "I need to fill a position, who is the most-qualified person for the job?" Tsk, tsk, tsk wrong framing.

The correct question is "I need to fill a position, where can I find a person of color?" Now at some level that is a good piece of the puzzle, and one should look for a pool of qualified people who can be reached out to. But they aim to go a step further and get back past equal opportunity to equal outcome, so you need to hire the Black person regardless.

As we previously noted, the different outcomes for Black people is a problem worthy of a national discussion about how to change them. However, saying White privilege has unfairly elevated all White people and now they should get out of the way is neither a viable nor sustainable solution. If it was not forbidden by the new definition, it would be called reverse racism.

Whiteness and White Privilege are simply ways to make achievement gaps the result of external forces and once we make race-consciousness a part of all systems and decisions, we can get to the equal outcomes that is their goal. The immense diversity in human skills and capabilities ensures that's impossible. Striving toward equal opportunity is a valiant cause, but not at the expense of using a new flavor of discrimination to ensure the result you want. It will take a deeper dive into root causes to achieve sustainable solutions.

CHAPTER 4- DEEP DIVE

This is where the other logical fallacy of White Fragility comes into play. It is the presumption of guilt, but worse than the usual legal version of this because no evidence other than the Whiteness and White skin of the accused need be presented. Even worse than that, there is no way to present any other evidence to the contrary because all protestations are deemed as proof of the racism that needs to be atoned for.

> "Despite its ubiquity, White superiority is also unnamed and denied by most Whites. If we become adults who explicitly oppose racism, as do many, we often organize our identity around a denial of our racially based privileges that reinforce racist disadvantage for others. What is particularly problematic about this contradiction is that White people's moral objection to racism increases their resistance to acknowledging their complicity with it. In a White supremacist context, White identity largely rests on a foundation of (superficial) racial tolerance and acceptance. We Whites who position ourselves as liberal often opt to protect what we perceive as our moral reputations, rather than recognize or change our participation in systems of inequity and domination." Pg. 109 White Fragility[33]

It is a truly insidious trick and the vast number of people who have willingly testified to their own unwitting demise is astonishing. She is saying that acknowledging racism is bad and even working to fight it is actually part of the problem. You must help tear down the system not just choose to act fairly toward all people.

This is not proof of the validity of the White Fragility argument or of the existence of systemic racism. It is proof that the indoctrination of this country with liberal beliefs, including liberal/White guilt, though our education system has succeeded.

In order to name all White people as racists you must first transform the definition of racism in two ways.

1. Racism can only be employed by the powerful against the powerless.
2. Racism does not require an action, simply that you benefit from its existence.

> "New racism is a term coined by film professor Martin
> Barker to capture the ways in which racism has
> adapted over time so that modern norms, policies,
> and practices result in similar racial outcomes as
> those in the past, while not appearing to be expli-
> citly racist." Pg. 39 White Fragility [34]

This allows it to be malign, but also invisible and therefore available anywhere it is needed to explain a problem or justify a needed transformation.

> "When a racial group's collective prejudice is backed
> by the power of legal authority and institutional
> control, it is transformed into racism, a far-reaching
> system that functions independently from the in-
> tentions or self-images of individual actors." Pg. 20
> White Fragility[35]

That is the trick right there, when you create a "racism" that doesn't require a belief or even an action, you have captured the entire group of White people in your net. And you can then proceed to teach them how to acknowledge their original sin and to atone for it by dismantling the system.

It should surprise no one that is the business Robin DiAngelo is in. She is an outrageously, highly-paid anti-racism consultant scoring tens of thousands of dollars per hour advising organizations and the White people in them how to properly bend the knee and how to empower and reward their Black employees for their troubles.

The idea of ubiquitous White racism is not just good for her business, it is good for power redistribution. It provides an easy explanation for Black performance lag while also satisfying the need to assuage liberal guilt. It also requires the current system be destroyed and the reins of power handed to the previously disadvantaged while being guided by enlightened souls like herself. She doesn't bother to address what will happen when these people, all having their own prejudices and biases, then control the levers of power. Will there be a need to teach them how to not abuse it and systemify a new, new racism?

Amazingly she even uses it to punish those who thought they were helping by living "color blind" lives where they treated everyone equally.

> "Because no one can actually be color blind in a racist
> society, the claim that you are color blind is not a
> truth; it is a false belief." Pg. 127 White Fragility[36]

Gotcha. She is right at some level because of course we all see color, but as conscious humans we can manage the next step and not make judgments about individuals based solely on the color of their skin. Ms. DiAngelo ignores this by using her explanation that merely being White in America erases your color-blind approach to people and requires that instead of judging them by the content of their character, you must judge them and treat them according to the color of their skin. Otherwise, by default, the racist system will discriminate against them.

"One line of King's speech in particular—that one day

he might be judged by the content of his character
and not the color of his skin—was seized upon by
the White public because the words were seen to
provide a simple and immediate solution to racial
tensions: pretend that we don't see race, and racism
will end." Pg. 41 White Fragility[37]

There you have it. Martin Luther King Jr.'s dream is canceled,
explicitly, disingenuously and inaccurately. I don't know how
much weight you can put on someone who writes about race and
fails to even correctly state, in an edited book nonetheless, that
King was not talking about himself.

"I have a dream that my four children will one day
live in a nation where they will not be judged by
the color of their skin, but by the content of their
character."[38]

She misconstrues him again by acting as if the call was to
"pretend that we don't see race, and racism will end." Not even
close! He dreams his kids will be judged on character not color. He
makes no claim this means pretending to not see race, only that
we use our moral and ethical compasses to avoid harmful judgments based on it.

This is a truly inconvenient concept when your goal is to convince all White people that there is an ingrained racism they need
not even exercise in order to benefit from. We must now see race
first and only and make our judgments based on that. Not value
judgments, but judgments to ensure equal outcome.

CHAPTER 4- CALLS TO ACTION

Stand up and don't be counted.

The key to White Fragility is convincing White people who thought they were the good guys to report themselves to the authorities and ask to be flogged. Their goal is to gather a critical mass of udeful idiots then use the riots and mobs as leverage to coerce changes in every system to produce equal outcomes. Don't play along; be sand in the gears; and, demand studies and proof before any changes are made.

Be careful and cautious.

This is dangerous because they have coopted Human Resources at your job, the petty bureaucrats in your local government, and many of the people who run the organizations you and your families belong to. They will accuse you of, you guessed it, racism.

Fortunately they have so devalued the word it really has lost its sting. But it is still a menace in some environments.

Tell them you love everyone and everything. Calmly point out that dissent is patriotic and you are just following their lead.

Stand up for individual Liberty.

It is the entire raison d'être for this country's existence. It is why we don't have to put up with pretentious foreign phrases to tell us we are free to live as we wish. They want to criminalize dissent from what they deem as the politically correct views. They are not the deciders of what is politically correct and they certainly have no right to self-proclaim themselves enforcers against thought crimes.

This is a core American value. We cannot let them destroy it. It stops them from simply doing things like issuing diktats about how many genders there are today and punishing those who dare bring science into the discussion.

Be a happy warrior.

I am a serial violator but this is vital. It can be emotionally gratifying to dream about being the one who stands up to the totalitarian thugs and gives them an intellectual beat down.Save these for maximum effect. The goal is to recruit new members to our side. Many people are put off by even the best rants and those who will be swayed by them are already on board.

So, have your best reasonable arguments ready and save the heavy weapons for special occasions.

CHAPTER FIVE THE
UNITED WHITE SUPREMACIST
STATES OF AMERICA

Bottom Line Up Front

T he final major claim of White Fragility is that America is a White supremacist country due to the combination of systemic racism in all its major institutions, inherent racism in its White citizens, and the White privilege they enjoy as a result. They say this requires a fundamental transformation of all major institutions to remove this inequity.

There are so many places where White Fragility is offensive, but calling America a White Supremacist nation may be the worst. No other country on Earth offers all its citizens the freedom, opportunity and equality America does. The concept of White Fragility requires a nation so riddled through and through with systemic racism that it must be demonized with the greatest slur of all. Otherwise, how can we convince its citizens to join in its destruction.

The country was founded when we declared "We hold these truths to be self-evident, that all men are created equal". A noble statement yet one that self-evidently was not fully enacted as proven by slavery and the lack of women's rights. The Constitution did not state we had formed a perfect union, but a "more perfect union". And it provided the framework that has allowed great strides and advancements in human liberty Perfect? No. Continually striving for a better tomorrow? Yes.

If you look at the arc of our moral universe as a country, it has absolutely bent toward justice. Women got the right to vote, slavery was abolished at great cost, and every day America and all Americans became more free. That is something we should always remember while bearing in mind there is always room for improvement.

The idea that in the 21st century America is a White Supremacist nation is just absurd and we are under no obligation to play along. In the White Fragility scheme, however, it is the final key to justifying a fundamental transformation. America itself is evil and must be remade in a racially conscious image. One where White people must become the oppressed because they are guilty of Living While White.

It would be hard to find an idea more fundamentally at odds with what makes America the exceptional nation. Doing what Ms. DiAngelo wants would create a racial ethno-state that would enshrine discrimination based on color as the legitimate method to achieve perfect outcomes among all races.

All people should be given the opportunity to try and achieve equal outcomes. The idea there is any genetic or other component that would stop Black people or anyone else from achieving equally is repugnant. But expecting equal outcomes is counter-scientific and guarantees hurt feelings.

Mandating equal outcomes is an evil game that should never be played by anyone, anywhere, anytime. Equal opportunity is the fair and legitimate goal and then let the chips fall where they may. If they are falling in too unequal a fashion, then we should look at root causes not just change the score and determine new winners.

CHAPTER 5- DEEP DIVE

"Being perceived as White carries more than a mere
racial classification; it is a social and institutional
status and identity imbued with legal, political,
economic, and social rights and privileges that are
denied to others." Pg. 24 White Fragility[39]

The most ridiculous part is the constant identification of this
massive entitlement and advantage that is solely the result of this
shadowy system whose individual functions need not even be
named. Again, disparate outcome is the only proof required to establish the rigged game.

There are so many other factors that influence outcomes and
opportunities. But rather than consider them, they are immediately reduced to the spoils of the racist system. If your parents
finished school, didn't marry until they had good jobs, didn't have
kids until they had saved for the future and taught you the same
values then you are benefitting from the White Supremacist state
and somehow this is the system Blacks are excluded from. These
traits are exercised individually and cannot be simply gifted
based on skin color.

Ms. DiAngelo ignores this basic tenet of living in a country
where life, liberty and the pursuit of happiness are legally protected for everyone and simply focuses on her White whale of
Whiteness. She posits a nice way to discount any positive personal traits or accomplishments because if they are achieved by a
White person, they are inherently invalid.

"However, a positive White identity is an impossible
goal. White identity is inherently racist; White

people do not exist outside the system of White supremacy." Pg. 149 White Fragility[40]

This is more circular reasoning to keep you on the path that leads always from Whiteness to White identity to White privilege to White supremacist society and thus to the unearned rewards of systemic racism.

> "Individual Whites may be "against" racism, but they still benefit from a system that privileges Whites as a group. David Wellman succinctly summarizes racism as "a system of advantage based on race. These advantages are referred to as White privilege, a sociological concept referring to advantages that are taken for granted by Whites and that cannot be similarly enjoyed by people of color in the same context (government, community, workplace, schools, etc.)". Pg. 24 White Fragility[41]

And yet they can, and are, by many people of color some of whom rise quite high and are very successful even to the point of a multi-term Black president. The record of achievement by many Blacks shows the advantages the author calls White privilege could also be called 'family values and personal responsibility' privilege.

This privilege crosses the color line. Brookings Institute published a report on the three norms that lead to success by poor people. They attempted to show there was still an achievement gap between Blacks and White when they adhered to the three following norms:

1. Graduate from high school
2. Maintain a full-time job or have a partner who does
3. Have children while married and after age 21, should they choose to become parents.

Despite their best efforts, Brookings actually reinforced the notion that these norms were a much larger factor than race when evaluating success rates.

Following the success sequence? Success is more likely if you're white.

> "White Americans are significantly more likely to demonstrate all three norms than Black Americans: about 65 percent compared to 45 percent."[42]

Yet, overall only 52% of Whites are in the middle class while 45% of Blacks are. When Brookings dug a bit deeper they found,

> "Among those who follow all three norms, Blacks are significantly less likely to reach the middle class than Whites who do the same. About 73 percent of Whites who follow all three norms find themselves with income above 300 percent of the federal poverty line for their family size, while only 59 percent of Blacks who adhere to all three norms fare equally well:"[43]

That shows that Blacks succeeded at 80% of the rate Whites did without adjusting for any other differences just by following the three identified norms. Even if there were no other differences to account for the 20% gap, that is hardly a ringing endorsement of a systemic racism and White supremacist society that stops Blacks while rewarding Whites.

It shows that if Blacks follow the pathways to success, they are much more likely to get there than not. And whatever barriers may exist in society, the ability to achieve is not proscribed for Blacks in any meaningful way.

CHAPTER 5- CALLS TO ACTION

Savagely attack the claim America is a White Supremacist nation.

It was bad enough redefining racism to make all White folks de facto racists and the Systemic Racism thing is awful although really smart, but claiming America is a White Supremacist nation is a slur too far. It will offend many people who were not going to argue too much about something passive like Systemic Racism. Calling America a White Supremacist nation will make plenty of folks say, "Hold on a minute there big shooter".

It reminds people of Nazis and skinheads and the kind of scum who really **are** racists and white supremacists. When the topic of White Fragility comes up, find a way to point out that Ms. Di-Angelo believes we are all complicit as White Supremacists.

Refuse to be called a White Supremacist.

Point out the actively evil nature of Supremacism. She uses that provocative term the same way she uses the rest i.e. you don't have to be actively White Supremacist but since the sum total = White Supremacist, then by default you become one.

Remind everyone in earshot how grotesque a smear that actually is and that people who throw slurs like that out wholesale are the real fascists.

CHAPTER SIX A WHITER SHADE OF FRAGILITY

Bottom Line Up Front

White Fragility says White people have created a country in which Whiteness is the natural state of things. Where belief in outmoded ideas like individualism and merit hurts Black people. It claims that society is based on Whiteness as the norm for physical attributes, cultural representations, and personal achievement. It must be overcome and replaced with a color-sensitive society and systems.

White Fragility also describes the supposed inability or refusal of White people to accept these realities. It then blames them for their angry reactions to being informed they are racist to the bone and benefit from systemic racism in a White supremacist country. Ya think?

I mean what complete losers to not embrace the shredding of all the good this country and many folks, White and other flavors have done. We are all expected to do so with a smile and apologize for being so racist about it. Ongoing and sadly necessary disclaimer: I'm not saying racism did not happen, was not important, did not affect the growth of this country, did not damage Black people and does not exist in some form today. All of those things are true, but the string of redefinitions and invented ills that Ms. DiAngelo has knitted into White Fragility does not exist in anything remotely resembling the web she wove.

She has made a painfully poor case for it if you are not already predisposed to share her views. But it is still dangerous to oppose them in the current political climate. You should be scared, because the stakes are high and your livelihood and reputation are at stake if you refuse to go along with your assigned role as the villain.

I'm more angry at having to write this book and talk at length about Whites and Blacks as if we were separate. The Left has driven a wedge between us based on color and wants us to be at odds. Sadly, they have been fairly successful at making us that way. Obviously, they would claim it is the result of all this systemic racism etc. But I think it is much more due to the academic and activist Left inventing identity politics and their grievance industry that requires victims.

They built entire academic departments to produce multi-syllabic gibberish they use as the supposed framework for this house of cards. The more I saw the boloney spouted by the Ministry of Wokeness, the less impressive any of it was. Now having journeyed through the Orwellian world of White Fragility, we'll look at the very few tangible examples of the White hierarchy she managed to name in her book.

It is not an impressive lot.

CHAPTER 6- DEEP DIVE

We have completed our tour of the separate parts of her ideology. If you can call something that is unscientific, unsupported by analysis, unhelpful un-rooted in reality an ideology. But aside from this yet un-identified systemic racism, what is she talking about.

> "In fact, when we try to talk openly and honestly about race, White fragility quickly emerges as we are so often met with silence, defensiveness, argumentation, certitude, and other forms of pushback. These are not natural responses; they are social forces that prevent us from attaining the racial knowledge we need to engage more productively, and they function powerfully to hold the racial hierarchy in place. These forces include the ideologies of individualism and meritocracy, narrow and repetitive media representations of people of color, segregation in schools and neighborhoods, depictions of Whiteness as the human ideal, truncated history, jokes and warnings, taboos on openly talking about race, and White solidarity." Pg. 8 White Fragility [44]

Here at least we have some specifics to examine, albeit overly broad and simply posited without any proof. Let's take a run at some of the things that "hold the racial hierarchy in place" anyhow.

Individualism

> "Briefly, individualism holds that we are each unique and stand apart from others, even those within our social groups...According to the ideology of indi-

vidualism, race is irrelevant. Of course, we do oc-
cupy distinct race, gender, class, and other positions
that profoundly shape our life chances in ways that
are not natural, voluntary, or random; opportunity
is not equally distributed across race, class, and
gender. On some level, we know that Bill Gates's
son was born into a set of opportunities that will
benefit him throughout his life, whether he is medi-
ocre or exceptional. Yet even though Gates's son has
clearly been handed unearned advantage, we cling
tightly to the ideology of individualism when asked
to consider our own unearned advantages." Pg. 9
White Fragility[45]

This is an essential building block of White Fragility, the re-
moval of success as a personal achievement. It must be reduced
to the inevitable outcome of a system designed to benefit some
and hurt others. How else can systemic racism explain the disparate outcomes if the individuals involved and the decisions they
made were allowed to be factors. As we saw when we looked at
whether a White supremacist state existed, there are many factors of personal responsibility and choice that can greatly affect
the relative success of people of all races.

"Whites also produce and reinforce the dominant narratives of society—such as individualism and mer-
itocracy—and use these narratives to explain the
positions of other racial groups. These narratives
allow us to congratulate ourselves on our success
within the institutions of society and blame others
for their lack of success." pg. 27 White Fragility[46]

Success is unearned and merely a narrative. This demeans
the accomplishments of some of our greatest Americans, Black
and White, who raised themselves from humble circumstances
through a combination of natural ability, relentless abundance

of effort, and a path of decisions that did not distract them from their goals.

This does not ignore that those who start with wealth and good surroundings have an advantage. Of course, they do. Expanding that advantage to be a universal White launching pad and limiting it to exclude Black participation is ridiculous.

There is plenty of legitimate discussion of a wealth gap between Blacks and Whites. It exists and is one of the most painful examples of disparate outcome. There are many studies that evaluate the reasons for this gap like this one from Mckinsey.

> "The widening racial wealth gap disadvantages black
> families, individuals, and communities and limits
> black citizens' economic power and prospects, and
> the effects are cyclical. Such a gap contributes to
> intergenerational economic precariousness: almost
> 70 percent of middle-class black children are likely
> to fall out of the middle class as adults."[47]

America would certainly be better off if Black families succeeded at the rates White ones do and then passed that wealth on to the next generation. We should be looking at ways to make that more possible and likely.

One of the more striking things about this McKinsey research is it does not even mention the massive difference between Blacks and Whites in children born to unmarried mothers as a cause.

In 2018, that percentage for Black children was 69.4% and for White children 28.2%[48]. That is a painful truth that must be part of any discussion about a wealth gap or success rates. While the White Fragilicists may try to blame systemic racism for this, it is hard to find a more personal decision about responsibility than parenthood.

The very idea Ms. DiAngelo uses to frame individualism makes it an excuse for success that was more due to systemic advantage. She refuses to allow the individual to be distinct from their herd. The real meaning of individualism which has made America the greatest country ever is quite well-described by Herbert Hoover in a book he wrote while serving as Secretary of Commerce in 1921. It describes a goal of producing a system most likely to support the individual and cognizant of the need to do that for all.

America was far from perfect when he did this and the system favored White males in a repugnant way. He acknowledges the need to continually learn and advance the cause of liberty and that is something America has demonstrably and continually done since the Founding.

American Individualism has recently been reissued by Hoover Press. An excerpt of the book appears below.

> "Individualism has been the primary force of American civilization for three centuries. It is our sort of individualism that has supplied the motivation of America's political, economic, and spiritual institutions in all these years. It has proved its ability to develop its institutions with the changing scene. Our very form of government is the product of the individualism of our people, the demand for an equal opportunity, for a fair chance.

> "What we need today is steady devotion to a better, brighter, broader individualism—an individualism that carries increasing responsibility and service to our fellows. Our need is not for a way out but for a way forward."

> "There are malign social forces other than our failures that would destroy our progress. There are the equal dangers both of reaction and radicalism. The perpetual howl of radicalism is that it is the sole voice

of liberalism—that devotion to social progress is its field alone. These men would assume that all reform and human advance must come through government. They have forgotten that progress must come from the steady lift of the individual and that the measure of national idealism and progress is the quality of idealism in the individual. The most trying support of radicalism comes from the timid or dishonest minds that shrink from facing the result of radicalism itself but are devoted to defense of radicalism as proof of a liberal mind. Most theorists who denounce our individualism as a social basis seem to have a passion for ignorance of its constructive ideals."

"We cannot ever afford to rest at ease in the comfortable assumption that right ideas always prevail by some virtue of their own. In the long run they do. But there can be and there have been periods of centuries when the world slumped back toward darkness merely because great masses of men became impregnated with wrong ideas and wrong social philosophies."[49]

Those goals and promises have been improved on and will continue to grow toward as equal a set of opportunities and level a playing field as we can devise. Will that produce equal outcomes? Probably not and we should not want it to have that most impossible and dangerous mandate. When we see disparate outcomes, we should be inquisitive as to their cause and aim to provide a helping hand to any who fall behind for whatever reason.

Media representations of people of color

It is certainly fair to note that for a considerable portion of the modern media age people of color were under-represented and played subordinate roles in film and television. But, if you have not seen a sea change in the past decade you are not paying attention.

In the top 100 films of 2018, Blacks had 16.9 percent of the roles while Whites dropped to 63.7 percent. At this point Blacks are actually over-represented compared to their percentage of the population which is only 13.6. Those numbers were 13.2 percent and 71.2 percent as recently as 2008.[50] And from the pre-civil rights era it has been an even greater transition.

Segregation in schools and neighborhoods

There is no institutional segregation in the U.S. at this point as it was banned more than half a century ago, but there are definite areas that are disproportionally White vs Black and vice versa. On the whole, those that are majority White have a higher standard of living, lower crime and better schools.

> "While 50 percent of black people live in high-poverty neighborhoods (those with higher than 30 percent poverty, this is true for only 10 percent of whites. Similarly, while 50 percent of white people live in low-poverty neighborhoods (those with less than 10 percent poverty, this is true for only 10 percent of black people."

This is another excellent example of a disparate outcome, but it's also another instance where systemic racism has not been proven to be the culprit.

The fact she uses segregation to describe this is a tell she has made her customary leap from symptom to diagnosis without performing any tests. One of the main causative factors named when discussing the wealth gap and other factors related to social and financial mobility is redlining.

The definition says:

"redlining is the systematic denial of various services
by federal government agencies, local governments
as well as the private sector either directly or
through the selective raising of prices.

The social justice version focuses on practices which led to
fewer Blacks being able to get home loans or credit. There are
many claims this was solely a racist tool to stop desegregation
and to keep Blacks out of predominantly White neighborhoods.

This paper from the Center for American Progress inadvert-
ently counters that representation:

Systemic Inequality: Displacement, Exclusion, and
Segregation
How America's Housing System Undermines Wealth Building
in Communities of Color

"For centuries, structural racism in the U.S. housing
system has contributed to stark and persistent racial disparities in wealth and financial well-being,
especially between Black and White households...
This report examines how government-spon-
sored displacement, exclusion, and segregation
have exacerbated racial inequality in the United
States."[51]

The report attempts to use racism as the catch all to explain
disparities but in almost every case the application of risk miti-
gation procedures by lenders is just as good or better an explanation. Looking far enough back, approximately 100 years, the use
of racial makeup of a neighborhood was one of the factors used to
rate credit-worthiness.

This undoubtedly had a racial component but it also has a
grounding in the fact that the great majority of those qualified to
buy homes at the time were White. They were unlikely to buy

homes in Black neighborhoods and that Blacks had higher default rates on mortgages. Thankfully, this is now a historical anomaly and the profit motive is far more prevalent as the driving force for lending decisions.

But the disparity in home ownership was significant and whatever the causes, attempts to close the gap were warranted.

The Community Reinvestment Act passed in 1977 was designed to ensure that Black communities received as much access to lending capital as possible.

> "The Community Reinvestment Act (CRA) was enacted
> in 1977 to prevent redlining1 and to encourage
> banks and savings associations (collectively, banks)
> to help meet the credit needs of all segments of their
> communities, including low- and moderate-income
> neighborhoods and individuals."[52]

This seems like a good idea and if it had been enacted and enforced in accordance with the stated legal purposes may have been a good policy. But it was also seen as a tool that could be used by government regulators to gain aggressive compliance and even undue risk in loan approval for Blacks by lenders.

"We're from the government and we're here to help" is said to be one of the scariest phrases one can hear. In this case that became a reality. This report from the Federal reserve bank of Chicago is instructive.

Trends in homeownership: Race, demographics, and income

> "In particular, we still find a remarkable 2.5 percentage
> point decline in the White.Black homeownership
> differential from 1995 to 1997. Thus, our results
> leave open the possibility that the regulatory
> changes of the mid-1990s are narrowing the
> White.Black gap in homeownership rates."[53]

What they are pointing out is that for the first 18-years under CRA from 1977 to 1995 the actual rate of home ownership by Blacks declined, but somehow from 1995 to 1997 it grew by 2.5%. What could account for such a change?

The answer is former President Bill Clinton. His economic team was hitting their stride and had decided to use the CRA as a major lever to increase Black home ownership. This was official policy and as such a completely legitimate use of executive authority.

Much of the impetus for this was what is commonly called the Boston Fed Study, where a group of Federal Reserve analysts looked at data from the Home Mortgage Disclosure Act of 1990. This was information on mortgage approvals for Whites and minorities in Boston which showed a significant disparity in denial rates between them of 2.7 to 1 in favor of White applicants.

This study concluded that it did not take into account significant factors such as financial status, employment, and neighborhood characteristics. Their report issued a much lower ratio but still one that showed a disparity.

Mortgage Lending in Boston: Interpreting HMDA Data

> "Including the additional information on applicant
> and property characteristics reduces the disparity
> between minority and White denials from the
> originally reported ratio of 2.7 to 1 to roughly 1.6
> to 1. This lowered number is still a 60% difference
> for minorities and was widely noted as a reason to
> do more stringent and active enforcement of the
> CRA."[54]

Further studies would show there were even more factors that had a major bearing on approval rates and further reduced the disparity especially among well and fully qualified applicants. For these applicants, there was actually no disparity by race.

The Role of Race in Mortgage Lending: Revisiting the Boston Fed Study

> "Overall, significant racial differentials exist only for "marginal" applicants and are not present for those with higher incomes or those with no credit problems. Thus, the claim that non-economic discrimination is a general phenomenon is refuted. Further, I can say little regarding the existence of discrimination among "marginal" applicants. To conclude that such discrimination exists, one must prove that the observed differences are not due to economic factors."[55]

That is someone who understands statistical analysis pointing out exactly why disparate outcome does not prove systemic racism. This whole study shows that when you dig down, there are other reasons.

But this had not slowed the efforts of the Clinton Administration to push on for equality of outcome in home ownership even if there was no discrimination present in the lending practices.

Memos found in the Clinton Presidential Library long after this show an unethical and reckless use of CRA compliance and certification as a way to increase lending beyond safe limits. Both pressure on banks by regulators including the possibility or refusals to approve mergers and acquisitions if the banks did not lean as far forward as the Clinton team wished. They met with and empowered partners like the activist group ACORN to act on their behalf:

Clinton Library's Doc Dump Reveals CRA Fueled Subprime Bubble
04/25/2014

"target merging firms with less-than-stellar records and to get the banks to agree to greater community investment as a condition of regulatory approval for the merger," White House aide Ellen Seidman wrote in 1997 to Clinton chief economist Gene Sperling."[56]

The public shaming and threats worked.

"Public disclosure of CRA ratings, together with the changes made by the regulators under your leadership, have significantly contributed to ... financial institutions ... meeting the needs of low- and moderate-income communities and minorities," Rubin gushed. "Since 1993, the number of home mortgage loans to African Americans increased by 58%, to Hispanics by 62% and to low- and moderate-income borrowers by 38%, well above the overall market increase."[57]

This is what led to the 2.5% increase in Black home ownership noted in the 1995 to 1997 time frame. It also meant banks were approving loans they would not have otherwise given to avoid adverse actions from government regulators, loans that White applicants with the same risk factors would have been denied. Since the market and math don't care about good intentions that eventually came back to bite us all in the form of the sub-prime mortgage crash of the early 2000s.

Did the Community Reinvestment Act (CRA) Lead to Risky Lending?

"The researchers use loan-level data on mortgage originations and performance for 1999 to 2009 from the Home Mortgage Disclosure Act, collected by the Federal Financial Institutions Examination

Council, and data from the Federal Reserve Bank of Chicago that contains information on CRA exams. They find that in the six quarters surrounding a CRA exam, lending by banks undergoing a CRA exam is 5 percent higher on average than lending by control-group banks. Using data that track loan performance, the authors also show that loans originated by treatment-group banks around CRA exams are 15 percent more likely to be delinquent one year after origination than loans originated by control-group banks. Thus the evidence shows that around CRA examinations, when incentives to conform to CRA standards are particularly high, banks not only increase lending rates but also appear to originate loans that are markedly riskier."[58]

The banks did what the Clinton Administration wanted and the number of loans classified as sub-prime began to skyrocket. Current New York Governor Andrew Cuomo was then serving as the youngest Secretary of Housing and Urban Development (HUD) ever and he was Clinton's point man in getting the federal loan guarantee programs Fannie Mae and Freddie Mac into the game.

"In 1992, Congress adopted the ironically named Federal Housing Enterprises Financial Safety and Soundness Act, also known as the GSE Act, giving HUD the authority to administer the legislation's affordable housing goals. The law required Fannie Mae and Freddie Mac, when they acquired mortgages from lenders, to meet a quota of loans to borrowers who were at or below the median income where they lived. At first, the quota was 30%, but HUD was authorized to raise the quota and over time it did, eventually requiring a quota of 56%. In those heady days, HUD was pleased with its work.

In 2000, for example, when then-HUD Secretary
Andrew Cuomo was raising the quota to 50%, the
agency actually sounded boastful about its role.
Describing the gains in homeownership that had
been made by low- and moderate-income families,
HUD noted: "most industry observers believe that
one factor behind these gains has been improved
performance of Fannie Mae and Freddie Mac under
HUD's affordable lending goals. HUD's recent in-
creases in the goals for 2001-03 will encourage the
GSEs to further step up their support for affordable
housing." Credit scores or down payments were not
relevant; only income and minority status would
satisfy the goals."[59]

These good intentions to reduce the disparate outcome in
Black home ownership led to the eventual collapse of the sub-
prime mortgage market and wiped out the dreams of more than a
quarter of a million Black home owners.

Foreclosures by Race and Ethnicity: The Demographics of a
Crisis

"Applying the share of completed foreclosures for each
demographic group from the 2005 – 2008 cohorts
to the 2 million foreclosures on owner-occupied
properties completed between 2007 and 2009, we
estimate that African-American and Latino families
have already lost 240,020 and 335,950 homes, re-
spectively, since the beginning of the crisis."[60]

All together the picture of systemic racism causing the disparate outcome in home ownership does not have much, if
any, evidence backing it. And the failure of direct government
intervention that led to the sub-prime mortgage collapse should
give question to anyone who thinks we can mandate equality of

outcome without consequences.

The few marginally substantive claims Ms. DiAngelo made to support her White Fragility thesis blew away like dust in the wind as soon as they were scrutinized at all. These are not systemic problems, they are issues that exist in any multi-racial, multi-cultural group of people. She provides no reason to believe they are systemic or racist.

CHAPTER 6- CALLS TO ACTION

Don't accept the guilt.

I doubt you were likely to, but White Fragility is based on creating a collection of ills for White people to feel bad about. This makes it easier to manipulate them into ceding power and control to the smarty pantses who will change everything for the better. That's an easy NO. A proper dislike for state power is a basic part of the organizational structures and yes, the systems that make this country exceptional. They want you to feel guilty Blacks aren't doing as well and then not notice while the Left simply adjusts for the outcomes they want. Don't!

Be collaborative.

State loudly that all people should be legally protected to have the equal chance to rise as high as their skills and effort take them. Ask if the Fragilicists have specific examples where opportunities are denied not just examples where the outcomes didn't match what their don't-call-them-quotas say they should be.

They won't.

Advocate for viable and sustainable solutions.

Rather than simply changing the score now and declaring new winners, suggest a long-term plan to fix root causes of disparate achievement is a better plan. This is a great place to point out how simply applying Systemic Racism as the cause of all our problems might feel good right now but won't keep Black kids in schools or help them grow up in two parent households.

And since those are universal indicators for success, maybe they ought to be part of the discussion. You can offer, "Now I realize that is just my White Privilege speaking". Ha, just seeing if you were paying attention. Never say that, never cave to the mob. If you're not a racist you have nothing to apologize for and you have every right to point out factors that affect success for all people.

CHAPTER SEVEN
ARMORING UP FOR THE COUNTER-REVOLUTION

Bottom Line Up Front

The forces of Wokeness pushing White Fragility, Anti-Racism and Social Justice are the ones who have truly gained a systemic hold on major U.S. institutions. They own academia and our education system and have successfully indoctrinated several generations of our children to believe their ideology. They produce what passes for our popular culture and dominate most of the permanent bureaucracy of our government.

It is now dangerous to oppose their diktats if you work for a major corporation, government or are in a position where public opinion can damage you. They have unleashed a Woke Mob which thirsts for opportunities to display its righteousness by destroying heretics. This will be an uphill battle and a long war.

We are divided and the Left has decided the bulk of our systems and institutions are polluted and must go. Their solution is for White people to admit this, accept their culpability, and grab a sledgehammer.

No! And given the unhinged nature of the attacks and demands I think we need to fight this out, preferably on the battleground of ideas. That means an end to the wanton destruction and violence being currently used by the Woke Mob to force compliance. It may seem to be working for them but any deals done at gun point are not valid. So, the battle must be met with factual ammunition like I have provided and be assured there is plenty more coming. This is just a basic load to get you started.

If you plan to enter the fray, gird your loins because this is not an academic exercise. This is a policy cage match and the Left has decided that eye-gouging and biting are no longer off limits. If you walk into the octagon, keep your head on a swivel and be prepared for every flavor of cheap shot and lie to come your way.

The other option is to learn as much as you can of the other side's plan and without engaging it head on become sand in the gears. This is a safer approach and no one should hold it against you. It takes different types of actions and actors to win the war. I will not lie; we will need all the help we can to overcome the decades long advantage the Left has in this fight.

The biggest advantage we have on the Right, is that we are right. Our ideas about what made America great at the founding and greater every day are still completely valid. That is not to say Leftist ideas are completely wrong, but they choose to back concepts like White Fragility putting their worst foot forward. Consequently, we're not in a position to go exploring for any common ground with them right now because they declared war in the United States of White Supremacist America.

That country does not exist. We must defend the one that does and the ideas that have given us this shining city on a hill. Once we defeat the current blitzkrieg, we can begin constructive talks on a cease fire and actual improvements to benefit everyone.

Let's fight this assault and make our case to all Americans that we are better off with the forces of personal liberty rather than those of state power.

CHAPTER 7- DEEP DIVE

The rationale for White Fragility is that White people do not want to take responsibility for their unearned rewards and the subsequent effect of disadvantaging Black people. If we have seen one thing repeatedly on this tour of the grievance industry, it's that there are almost no actual verifiable facts the grievances are based on. Therefore, we should not accept them, let alone act on them.

There is plenty of disparate outcome showing that Whites outperform Blacks in many areas, but so do Latinos and let's not even bring Asians into this, because they outperform everyone in ways that are hard to fathom if racism is so systemic. Apparently, the system is fine-tuned enough to somehow avoid slowing Asians down and is only marginally effective on Latinos.

So, if there is no systemic racism undergirding a White Supremacist society, maybe the entire idea that getting mad when someone calls you a racist, which Ms. DiAngelo has branded White Fragility, is actually a perfectly normal and appropriate reaction to being called a horrific smear based on absolutely no evidence.

Perhaps a better term for it would be Whiteous Indignation because if you are labelled one of the most heinous insults in the playbook today, being Whiteously Indignant is perfectly understandable and not an example of some mythical fragility.

The ubiquity of this unsubstantiated serial insult to our decency and intelligence is a truly alarming thing. You cannot avoid someone on the anti-racist Left informing you of your sin and prescribing a self-flagellating trip down the fragility path to atone. But not just atone, for you must participate in this ul-

timately unhelpful attempt to try and install equality of outcome.

Attacking the status quo with White Fragility on race is just
a test case for using it to force a guilt-driven redistribution of
wealth and ultimately a socialized system complete with totalitarian power. This is their true goal. Racial issues are a great place
to start because slavery is such a heinous crime. The original sin
of the Founding cannot be erased without erasing all of the institutions it led to. Disparate outcomes prove the stain still exists
and so a hefty dose of White Out to erase the Whiteness is needed.

Government, finance, language, heritage...all must go. Education would have been added but that is already so wholly owned
and operated by the Ministry of Wokeness that it no longer even
pretends to educate, just indoctrinate. But all the rest? They say
burn 'em down and replace them with Ministries dedicated to ensuring the socialist-prescribed outcomes.

The systemic part of systemic racism leads to the inevitable
need to destroy and rebuild America. That is a feature not a bug in
their plan for a new socialist(ish) super state.

The reaction must be the same for every attempt by the Left
to force compliance: Never cave to the mob, never ever cave to
the mob, never. But that's not easy or even possible in a country
where every corporation seems to be competing to see who can
bend the knee most completely. The danger in choosing not to is
real and can be career-ending. Cancel Culture can come for anyone
and it has a Salem Witch Trials feel, or maybe more accurately a
Monty Python and the Holy Grail witch-burning scene where the
mob accuses the woman of being a witch and is very keen to burn
her.

> VILLAGER #1: We have found a witch, might we burn her?
> CROWD: Burn her! Burn!
> BEDEVERE: How do you know she is a witch?
> VILLAGER #2: She looks like one.

BEDEVERE: Bring her forward.
WITCH: I'm not a witch. I'm not a witch.
BEDEVERE: But you are dressed as one.
WITCH: They dressed me up like this.
CROWD: No, we didn't -- no.
WITCH: And this isn't my nose, it's a false one.
BEDEVERE: Well?
VILLAGER #1: Well, we did do the nose.
BEDEVERE: The nose?
VILLAGER #1: And the hat -- but she is a witch!
CROWD: Burn her! Witch! Witch! Burn her!

Their rules regarding heresy are not well-defined and are undergoing constant change. One of the first thought crimes identified was to proclaim "All Lives Matter" when confronted with the maxim "Black Lives Matter". It is a simple truth and one would think unassailable concept which should prompt the response "well of course they do, but we are primarily concerned with disparate outcomes for Blacks right now". Instead it has become essentially a hate crime to bring it up and could well land you on the wrong side of your HR staff and the door to your work if you're not careful. It could even get you shot as it did for one young woman when she said, "All Lives Matter."

For many, an outright refusal to play along may not be a viable option. So, here is a list of ways to feign, if not full submission, at least the appearance of compliance. A "keeping your job so you can live to fight another day" solution. After that we'll have the FU answer book for arguments where you face no jeopardy or for the few, we happy few, we band of brothers and sisters who choose to fight and say damn the consequences.

Start by repeating this again and again until it is a reflexive mantra.
Never cave to the mob.
Ever!

Once you do, they are like piranhas smelling blood in the water and they will try to devour you. You may have made a callous statement or an unkind remark or God forbid told a non-PC joke at some point in the past 50 years. They will tell you the only way to atone for this is to submit to their tender mercies and admit this is proof you are the racist they knew you were all along.

Don't do it.
Never cave to the mob.

You can admit you were an imperfect person who has strived to grow and improve yourself, but do not accept their premise that any imperfect thoughts or deeds are proof of your evil Whiteness. And don't ever accept their larger premise that your participation is not required to be a modern racist. That all you had to do to require their judgment is the crime of living while White.

This is gobsmackingly ironic and hypocritical coming from a movement that popularized the idea that Driving While Black is a national epidemic. But we can't get sidetracked by their incoherence because it is pervasive.

Now that we have established our one bedrock principle which is immutable
What was it again?
That's right:
Never cave to the mob!

But then what? You just became some flavor of pariah and the mob will be circling you looking for a weakness to exploit. Don't think you are armored up yet, you have many vulnerabilities and you must be prepared for unscrupulous and immoral attacks.

They will go after your livelihood by informing your employer of your unrepentant racism, or if you are an entrepreneur by informing your customers they support racism if they patronize you. They will attack your friends and family and yes, even your kids. That is if they haven't already coopted your kids as the attack vector themselves.

This is one of their most insidious tactics and it comes right out of every totalitarian manual. Indoctrinate the kids in state-controlled schools and use them against the reactionary beliefs of their parents. They eventually get to the point of using the kids as informants to root out the non-compliant. We have seen evidence of this already with schools, doctors and other parents asking kids if there are guns in their home. Soon they will be doing racism health checks.

Now we come to that fork in the road: fight or fake it. Will you actively oppose the anti-racism agenda and the larger social justice transformation they are bringing. Or will you present at least the appearance of compliance. Many will have to go along to get along, because the consequences for heresy are staggering. No judgment here.

If you are not going to just tell them to pound sand, then say things like "That's very interesting, I'd like to learn more". Because these well-meaning totalitarians don't think that's what they are. They think they are enlightened missionaries bringing the good word to backwards troglodytes who know no better. Indulge them and let them share their wisdom. Ask innocuous questions like "How does that work?" and "Where does that information come from?" But seriously, be careful with even that because they don't think there is anything to question so they may sense your dissident status.

Then get your children out of public schools. If you don't, you will be fighting a constant retrograde battle against state-sponsored indoctrination of anti-racism and the rest of the social justice Wokeness ideology. Even if you win, they will have infiltrated mountains of this into their heads and some will inevitably stick.

How to replace the systemic indoctrination of the public schools is the biggest challenge facing us as we oppose this but that is a much larger topic for another day. Just flee now and find appropriate alternatives like charter schools or home schooling.

You cannot escape this agenda but the more you know and the less you expose yourself and your family to it without a reality check the better. Start by knowing it is not based on science or facts and there are principled, logical refutations of their claims. The ones you read in all the previous chapters should make you more confident in your refusal to go along with their plans for your reeducation and our country's fundamental transform- ation.

Now for the fighting wing. You're well aware of the dangers and you're choosing to march toward the sound of gunfire anyhow. Good! The best part of this is you already know how to play this game but let's go over some safety tips and tactics.

Don't say anything they can construe as racist. And I heard all of you just say "But they claim everything we say is racist no matter what?' You're right, they do and it's BS. We can't change that. But whatever your mindset is going into this, if your plan is to fight a race-based battle. You just read the wrong book.

If your goal is to fight a "race-based policies are un-American" battle, we're on the same team. Arm yourself with facts and there are a ton of them in the previous chapters. Do better than that, read the source materials. Read the smartest people on the other side. I just paused while most of you earnestly said, 'There aren't any". I would agree by the standard of smart that means not be- lieving and propagating ridiculous things like White Fragility. Keep in mind what Ronald Reagan said, "The trouble with our Lib- eral friends is not that they're ignorant, it's just that they know so much that isn't so".

Pick the most-widely accepted big brains from the Left on this topic or any other and read their argument, check their sources, then go back to the smart people on our side to find the best de- molition of their silliness.

Be prepared to agree with some things to establish common ground before you deploy your factual and rhetorical heavy weapons. Disparate outcomes for Black people in America is real and we should all want to change it. Say that. It's easy because it's true. Say you want all people to share equally in the opportunities available and the fruits of their own labors without any artificial restraints. Again, easy because it's true.

Then say, "I oppose policies designed to create equal outcomes because they punish those who achieve more based on their own skill and effort". Then ask them what they think are the best ways to create more opportunities. That is the real crux of the entire disagreement between Right and Left they want state control and we want personal liberty.

They see that equal opportunity intrinsically creates unequal outcomes and they want to "fix" that. We see unequal outcomes as a chance for the best and brightest to excel and gain more based on the sweat of one's own brow. We are willing to sacrifice to ensure that we do not stop our own success with acts or inactions that damage our chances. They want to game the scores to get a "fair" result unfairly.

Coupling that belief system with a good-hearted understanding that we should also put some of our energy and rewards into improving the system so those who are striving but not succeeding can up their outcomes. All the while, recognizing that disparate outcomes are the inevitable result given the varied skills and circumstances inherent in each of us.

This is actually a pretty good description of the strong and vibrant America our country is today. The liberty and opportunity available to every American has continually increased since the Founding. Let's be proud of it and aim to keep that progress, which is unequaled in human history, rising.

CHAPTER 7- CALLS TO ACTION

Don't let fear paralyze you.

Yes, the stakes are high. Fear is a valid emotion and this is an opportunity to act in the face of fear courageously. You are needed in the arena as Teddy Roosevelt said in his 1910 speech Citizenship in a Republic.

"It is not the critic who counts; not the man who points out how the strong man stumbles, or where the doer of deeds could have done them better. The credit belongs to the man who is actually in the arena, whose face is marred by dust and sweat and blood; who strives valiantly; who errs, who comes short again and again, because there is no effort without error and shortcoming; but who does actually strive to do the deeds; who knows great enthusiasms, the great devotions; who spends himself in a worthy cause; who at the best knows in the end the triumph of high achievement, and who at the worst, if he fails, at least fails while daring greatly, so that his place shall never be with those cold and timid souls who neither know victory nor defeat."

Be smart and pick your battles.

Racism is a war zone. Every time you poke your White head up to say something, there's a Lefty zealot sniper waiting to take a shot at you. But if we do nothing, they will destroy this country. So get in the fight and keep your head on a swivel.

Defend America.

The United States is not riddled with Systemic Racism and is certainly not a White Supremacist Nation. It's crucial to oppose and vanquish this ludicrousness. If you are not a racist, then saying you're not racist does not make you fragile. Unleash your Whiteous Indignation and be insulted at the idiocracy of White Fragility. Fight the good fight smartly. Only when we stop this nonsense, will we be able get on to an actual national discussion on race based on facts not feelz.

THE FINAL COUNTDOWN

A merica is not a White Supremacist country rife with systemic racism and all white people are not racist. It should never have taken this many pages and points to get to those painfully simple conclusions, but we live in crazy times. Plus, I wanted to give you a bunker full of ammo to shoot holes in the outrageous smears and claims being made by people waving a copy of White Fragility around like it means something.

It does, but not what they say it does. It is the perfect example of the Wokeness virus spreading to hosts with weaknesses that make them easy to infect. It is the culmination of decades of academic efforts to create a philosophy/ideology that will allow them to begin dismantling this country. They think America is evil and feel empowered to say that out loud.

Good. Because everyone needs to hear what they really think and what they want to do, because it is awful.

Make no mistake, it's socialism. They may dress it up with some better branding, or might not because they are really feeling full of themselves because they are winning. That's right, winning. It's not over yet and that is the purpose of starting this series. We are not going to lose to a bunch of pampered, over-educated, under-productive, parasitical, oxygen thieves.

The Wokeness Mob and their Social Justice shock troops are riding high right now. Cities are burning, people are caving to their demands, statues are being toppled, and America's history is being erased. But they can't just edit the Constitution and they can't brainwash all of us. We are the fighting few and even in the face of overwhelming odds we will turn back those who wish to topple America and the American values that make this the greatest country in the world.

Normal Americans have seen their country, their heritage and their flag being burnt and trodden upon by disrespectful punks with zero accomplishments but a list of grievances and demands a mile long. Well the time has come to say No More!

The counter-attack has begun and this book is the first Freedom Manual. More FM's are on the way. We will take apart their entire totalitarian power grab, stupid idea by stupid idea. Some upcoming topics will be: "The Grievance Industry: How the Left convinces privileged people they're oppressed";" Canceling Free Speech: Shut up they said, Hell No we answered"; "The Second Amendment: You can have my guns when I run out of ammo and am lying dead on top of a mountainous pile of empty shell casings" (working title).

I think you get the idea, we're mad as Hell. They drew the battle lines; we will win this war. It will be ugly, but much uglier would be the Socialist States of America. So, strap on your anti-Wokeness armor, load up your rhetoric rifles, and let's take this country back.

---

[1] Critique of the Gotha Programme, Karl Marx, 1875

[2] 1984, George Orwell, Pg. 139

[3] Wage Labour and Capital, Karl Marx, 1847

[4] "The Role of the Chinese Communist Party in the National War" (October 1938), Selected Works, Vol. II, p. 202.

[5] Communist Manifesto, Marx & Engels, 1848

[6] Declaration of Independence, July 1776

[7] U.S. Constitution, 14th Amendment, Section 1

[8] "On the People's Democratic Dictatorship" (June 30, 1949), Selected Works, Vol. IV, p. 418.

[9] Pg. 1 White Fragility, Robin DiAngelo [Kindle edition]

[10] Ibid, Ibid, Ibid, Ibid

[11]

[12]

[13]

[14] Race as a factor in police homicides. Security Studies group White paper June 2020, Dr. Brad Patty & Jim Hanson

[15] Pg. 30 White Fragility, Robin DiAngelo [Kindle edition]

[16] Pg. 30 White Fragility, Robin DiAngelo [Kindle edition]

[17] Explaining Discrepancies in Arrest Rates Between Black and White Male Juveniles

Paula J. Fite, Porche' Wynn, and Dustin A. Pardini

https://www.ncbi.nlm.nih.gov/pmc/articles/PMC2981137/

[18] USA Today June 15, 2020, N'dea Yancey-Bragg, What is systemic racism? Here's what it means and how you can help dismantle it

[19] Ibid.

[20] Washington Post, June 12, 2020, Ruth Marcus, If you don't believe systemic racism is real, explain these statistics

[21] The Real Root Causes of Violent Crime: The Breakdown of Marriage, Family, and Community, March 17, 1995 Patrick Fagan

[22] Why Does Racial Inequality Persist? Culture, Causation, and Responsibility Glenn C. Loury

May 7, 2019

[23] Pew Research Center June 12, 2020 Amid Protests, Majorities Across Racial and Ethnic Groups Express Support for the Black Lives Matter Movement

[24] Pg. 17 White Fragility, Robin DiAngelo [Kindle edition]

[25] Critical Han Studies, The History, Representation, and Identity of China's Majority

Mark Elliott Pg. 177

[26] Uppercasing Black New York Times Dean Baquet and Phil Corbett June 30, 2020

[27] Pg. 19 White Fragility, Robin DiAngelo [Kindle edition]

[28] Ibid.

[29] Pg. 9 White Fragility, Robin DiAngelo [Kindle edition]

[30] Ibid.

[31] Pg. 4 White Fragility, Robin DiAngelo [Kindle edition]

[32] Ibid.

[33] Pg. 109 White Fragility, Robin DiAngelo [Kindle edition]

[34] Ibid.

[35] Ibid.

[36] Pg. 127 White Fragility, Robin DiAngelo [Kindle edition]

[37] Ibid.

[38] Martin Luther King Jr. Aug. 28, 1963 "I have a Dream" speech

[39] Pg. 24 White Fragility, Robin DiAngelo [Kindle edition]

[40] Ibid.

[41] Pg. 24 White Fragility, Robin DiAngelo [Kindle edition]

[42] Following the success sequence? Success is more likely if you're white. Richard V. Reeves, Edward Rodrigue, and Alex Gold Thursday, August 6, 2015

[43] Ibid.

[44] Pg. 8, White Fragility, Robin DiAngelo [Kindle edition]

[45] Ibid.

[46] Ibid.

[47] The economic impact of closing the racial wealth gap, Nick Noel, Duwain Pinder, Shelley Stewart, and Jason Wright August 13, 2019

[48] National Vital Statistics Reports Volume 68, Number 13 November 27, 2019

[49] Herbert Hoover American Individualism 1922

[50] Inequality in 1,200 Popular Films: Examining Portrayals of Gender, Race/ Ethnicity, LGBTQ & Disability from 2007 to 2018. Dr. Stacy L. Smith, Marc Choueiti, Dr. Katherine Pieper, Kevin Yao, Ariana Case & Angel Choi, September 2019

[51] Systemic Inequality: Displacement, Exclusion, and Segregation How America's Housing System Undermines Wealth Building in Communities of Color, Danyelle Solomon, Connor Maxwell, and Abril Castro August 7, 2019,

[52] Community Reinvestment Act, Office of the Comptroller of the Currency, March 2014

[53] Trends in homeownership: Race, demographics, and income, Lewis M. Segal and Daniel G. Sullivan June 1998

[54] Mortgage Lending in Boston: Interpreting HMDA Data, Alicia H. Munnell, Lynn Elaine Browne, James McEneaney, and **Geoffrey M.B. Tootell**

[55] The Role of Race in Mortgage Lending: Revisiting the Boston Fed Study by Raphael W. Bostic Division of Research and Statistics Federal Reserve Board of Governors, December 1996

[56] Clinton Library's Doc Dump Reveals CRA Fueled Subprime Bubble Investors Business Daily Editorial 04/25/2014

[57] Ibid.

[58] Did the Community Reinvestment Act (CRA) Lead to Risky Lending? (NBER Working Paper No. 18609), **Sumit Agarwal**, **Efraim Benmelech**, **Nittai Bergman**, and **Amit Seru**

[59] Five Years Later: Don't Mention the Feds Peter J. Wallison, Wall Street Journal, Sept. 17, 2013

[60] Foreclosures by Race and Ethnicity: The Demographics of a Crisis CRL Research Report, Debbie Gruenstein Bocian, Wei Li, and Keith S. Ernst, June 18,

2010

[61] Citizenship in a Republic, Theodore Roosevelt, 1910 speech at the Sorbonne, Paris

ABOUT THE AUTHOR

Jim Hanson

Jim is President of Security Studies Group a next generation national security and foreign policy shop specializing in information operations. He served in US Army Special Forces and conducted Counter-Terrorism, Counter-Insurgency and Humanitarian operations in more than a dozen countries.

He is the author of Cut Down the Black Flag – A Plan to Defeat the Islamic State. He has appeared as a guest on multiple FOX News programs, CNN, MSNBC, ABC, BBC, Al Jazeera, Deutsche Welle, C-Span, and numerous national radio shows.

Made in the USA
Middletown, DE
11 April 2021